EARLY TIMES
THE STORY OF
ANCIENT ROME

Suzanne Strauss Art

(The Fay School, Southborough, Massachusetts)

WAYSIDE PUBLISHING
CONCORD, MASSACHUSETTS

To Bob

ISBN 1-877653-23-3

ITED IN THE UNITED STATES

Acknowledgements

I am greatly indebted to my colleague, Richard Upjohn of the History Department at the Fay School. He thoughtfully examined two separate drafts of my manuscript, drawing upon his impressive knowledge of ancient history to question the accuracy of particular data and to suggest additional materials that might enrich the text in general. Thank you, Dick, for supporting my project from the start and for helping me to progress from a hesitant first draft to a well-verified first edition.

Thanks also go to colleague Daniel Arnaud, teacher of Classics at Fay, who read an early draft of the manuscript and offered useful constructive criticism. His insights about the ancients—often humorous and fanciful—have helped me to keep the more ponderous aspects of my *magnum opus* in proper perspective.

An essential step in preparing my various manuscripts for publication is the conversion of floppy discs to hard ones. My good friend, Professor Stephen Van Evera, has cheerfully pressed his computer into service for this task on numerous occasions, even providing a special box of discs for my projects. Thanks, Steve!

I am grateful to my publisher, David Greuel, for his patience and thoroughness while helping me to prepare the proofs of the book for the printer. The confidence he originally expressed in the viability of my series of books provided me with the boost I needed to forge each early draft into a finished product.

Most of all, love and appreciation go to my ever-supportive family—my husband Bob and my children David and Robyn.

The photographs in this book have been reproduced with the permission of the Boston Museum of Fine Arts. Drawings are by the author.

List of Maps

To The Teacher

THE STORY OF ROME is the third in a series of books on ancient cultures geared for middle school students (grades 5-8). It can serve as the basis of a year's course or a shorter unit study.

The EARLY TIMES series is the product of eight years of teaching ancient history to middle school students as well as a life-long fascination with the subject. I was motivated to write my own material almost at the beginning of my teaching career, since I could find no book that adequately presented the information I wanted my students to learn. Textbooks tend to cover a large number of civilizations in a superficial and homogenized manner, while a trade book focuses upon a specific feature of a culture. What I needed was a series of texts, each of which presented a comprehensive overview of a particular ancient civilization (namely, Egypt, Greece, and Rome) and then delved into the meatier aspects of religion, art, science, cuisine, political intrigue, and so forth. Furthermore, the books had to be written in a style that would appeal to middle school students, stimulating their interest and enticing them to read further. Since I knew of no such series, I decided to write one myself, basing it upon my own scholarly research as well as the plethora of materials I have gathered for my classroom. My students at Fay School have been active participants in the development of EARLY TIMES, and the series highlights those issues and activities that they enjoyed the most.

THE STORY OF ROME begins with the legend of Romulus and Remus and ends with the dethronement of the Emperor Romulus Augustulus in AD 476. It depicts the evolution of Roman civilization from a small cluster of villages along the Tiber to a vast empire, all the while focusing upon the more succulent details of day-to-day life in an effort to make Rome "come alive" for middle school readers. An emphasis is placed upon vocabulary, particularly the Latin roots from which so many of our English words are derived. At the end of every chapter are questions to help the students review what they have just read. "Ideas to Think About" provide material for further discussion and/or enrichment activities, while "Projects" include suggestions for independent or group research assignments. The books listed in SUGGESTED READINGS are excellent resources for research projects, and their colorful illustrations are very useful for enriching class discussions. I recommend that a number of these books be available to the students in the classroom throughout their study of Rome.

I welcome any constructive criticism relating to the book, and I would be glad to consider those suggestions for projects and activities that might enhance the next edition of THE STORY OF ANCIENT ROME.

Contents

PART THREE — THE EMPIRE

TIMELINE OF MAJOR EVENTS

(Note: The letter c stands for circa, a Latin word meaning around. Therefore, c 850 BC means around 850 BC.)

Beginnings

c 2000 BC	Earliest Indo-European invasions
c 850	Arrival of Etruscans
c 750	Greek colonies in Sicily and southern Italy
753	Legendary founding of Rome
625	Union of villages becomes the city of Rome
509	Tarquinius Superbus driven out
	Founding of the Republic

The Republic

494	The plebeians go on strike
493	The first two tribunes are appointed
c 450	The Twelve Tables
390	The Gauls sack Rome
264-241	First Punic War
218-202	Second Punic War
146	Destruction of Carthage
133	Murder of Tiberius Gracchus
123	Murder of Gaius Gracchus
107	Marius becomes consul, begins army reforms
82-80	Dictatorship of Sulla
70	Consulship of Pompey and Crassus
60	First Triumvirate
59	Consulship of Caesar
58-50	Caesar's conquest of Gaul
49-44	Civil Wars, Dictatorship of Caesar
44	Murder of Caesar
43	Second Triumvirate
31	Battle of Actium

The Empire

27 BC-AD 14	Principate of Augustus
AD 1	Birth of Christ
14-68 AD	Julio-Claudian Emperors
79	The Colosseum is opened
79	Eruption of Mt. Vesuvius
96-180	Five Good Emperors
248	1000th birthday of Rome
270-275	Aurelian (restoration of unity)
284-305	Diocletian comes to power and splits the Empire in two
305-337	Rule of Constantine
379-392	Theodosius is Emperor of the East
392-395	Empire is united under Theodosius
394	Christianity becomes the state religion
410	Alaric sacks Rome
455	The Vandals invade Rome
476	Romulus Augustulus is deposed
527-565	Rule of Justinian in the East
1453	Constantinople is conquered by the Turks

fig. 1 — **Italy and Sicily**

INTRODUCTION

What do you think of when you hear the word "Roman?" Swashbuckling swordsmen? Fearless gladiators? Lightning-fast chariots racing around hairpin turns? These images are certainly part of the story of Rome, and they provide lively entertainment in movie theaters. But there was much more to the rich Roman civilization that flourished around the Mediterranean Sea over two thousand years ago.

The rule of law, for example. Did you know that the system of laws devised by the Romans to protect the rights of citizens worked so well that it became a cornerstone of our own judicial process? Then there's the matter of government. The Roman Empire was immense: It gradually expanded from one small village until it covered two million square miles and had a population of over sixty million people! The Roman way of life endured throughout this vast realm for centuries largely because a very efficient network of government officials kept everything running smoothly. In fact, our Founding Fathers used the Roman framework of government as a model when they drafted the US Constitution in the eighteenth century.

Who were the Romans? They were a serious-minded, industrious, and highly disciplined people of the ancient world who had a genius for making the most of every situation. They struggled hard to attain their goals, yet they were flexible enough to understand the value of compromise. When they expanded their domain, they allowed the people they conquered to retain many of their local traditions. They even made allies of their former enemies. This practice was unheard of in those early times, and it was a key to Rome's success in ruling a huge and diverse population. The Romans genuinely respected the cultural achievements of other societies, particularly the Greeks; they eagerly embraced those new ideas and customs that they found appealing, adapted them to meet their own needs, and later spread the Romanized versions of those concepts throughout their empire.

The story of ancient Rome is filled with political drama, military exploits, and fascinating personalities. How do we know so much about it? Fortunately, the Romans left us numerous records of their remarkable civilization. For example, they loved legends, and we can still read about their superheroes who embodied the traits they valued most:

patriotism, courage, and moral integrity. The writings of Roman historians provide us with thoughtful descriptions of everyday life as well as careful analyses of the major political events of particular eras. Lifelike statues and colorful paintings enable us to clearly visualize the men, women, and children who lived and laughed in those ancient cities and towns, while the ruins of temples, amphitheaters, and aqueducts dramati-cally attest to the ingenuity of Roman engineers. Finally, the rediscovery of the ancient cities of Pompeii and Herculaneum has brought to light the fascinating remains of entire communities that were frozen in time nearly twenty centuries ago.

The Geography of Italy

Our study of the Romans starts with a short geography lesson. Modern Rome is the capital of Italy, a country occupying a long, narrow peninsula in southern Europe that juts into the Mediterranean Sea. Look at the map on page viii. Doesn't Italy look like a high-heeled boot that is kicking a football? The "football" is the island of Sicily, which lies 20 miles southwest of the "boot." The Italian peninsula is 683 miles long, and it measures 155 miles at its widest point. About one hundred miles south of Sicily is the coast of Africa. Look at the map on page 3.

Notice that Italy is right at the center of the Mediterranean basin. We will learn how this strategic location played a crucial role in the expansion of the early Roman Empire.

The Adriatic Sea separates the east coast of Italy from the nations that once made up Yugoslavia. Off the west coast of the peninsula is the Tyrrhenian Sea, and beyond are the islands of Corsica and Sardinia. Today Sardinia belongs to Italy and Corsica is a part of France. The Ionian Sea lies between the heel of Italy and the western coast of Greece. All of these seas—the Adriatic, the Tyrrhenian, and the Ionian—are arms of a larger body of water, the Mediterranean Sea.

Three quarters of the Italian peninsula is mountainous. While the Alps tower majestically along the northern border, the Apennine Mountains run from northwest to southeast along the spine of Italy. Although the rugged limestone of the Apenines casts sharp outlines against the sky, the mountains never rise above 10,000 feet. Numerous volcanoes have erupted in Italy over the last several thousand years. The best known are Mount Vesuvius, on the southwestern coast (it is still active), and Mount Etna on Sicily.

To the west of the Apennines are the wide, coastal plains of Etruria, Latium, and Campania; the rich, volcanic soil of these regions is ideal for growing crops. The land to the east of the mountains is drier and less fertile, and it has been used as pastureland since earliest times.

The largest rivers in Italy are the Po, the Arno, and the Tiber. They flow through wide fertile valleys, but their low water levels make them unnavigable. Some smaller rivers actually dry up in the summer! There are few good natural harbors along the Italian coast, a condition which discouraged the earliest settlers from seeking their living from the sea as the ancient Greeks had done. The best harbors are located toward the bottom of the "boot."

Italian summers are hot and dry, and the winters are mild and rainy (with snow in the high mountains). This temperate climate enables the farmers to plant their seeds in the fall; these slowly germinate during the winter months, and the crops are harvested in the spring before the summer heat dries them out. (Olives and grapes, however, are gathered in the fall.)

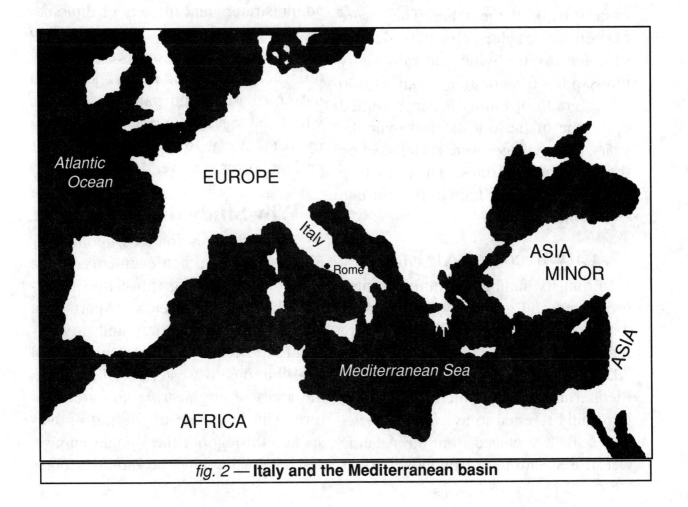

*fig. 2 — **Italy and the Mediterranean basin***

The Early Settlements

Around 1000 BC nomads (wandering herdsmen) from northeastern Europe began to settle on the plain of Latium in central Italy. They were part of a huge migration of people called the Indo-Europeans. Latium stretches from the Tiber River southward to the Volscian Hills and covers about 700 square miles. The newcomers came to be known as the Latins (dwellers of Latium).

Sixteen miles inland from the sea, seven hills rise dramatically above the eastern bank of the Tiber. They were carved out of deposits of volcanic sediment by the wind and rain many thousands of years ago. In about 800 BC, a group of Latin clansmen settled upon one of these hills, and over the years, other villages were established on the neighboring ones. These hilltop villages eventually united to form one city: Rome.

A City Becomes An Empire

From its humble beginning, Rome prospered and gradually extended its territory until it controlled the entire Italian peninsula. By the second century AD, the Roman Empire encircled the Mediterranean Sea, which the Romans arrogantly referred to as *Mare Nostrum* (our sea). It stretched from the Atlantic Ocean eastward to the Euphrates River and from the African deserts northward to the highlands of Britain and the forests of Germany. At its height, the empire encompassed forty-three provinces on the continents of Asia, Europe and Africa. (See the map on page 126.)

The Romans were not the first to rule over a huge empire. Indeed, the Egyptians, the Persians, and the Greeks (under the command of Alexander the Great) had conquered huge territories in the past. However, as we have already learned, the Romans were practical administrators and masters of diplomacy: By incorporating the people they conquered into their own culture, they ultimately established a vast and unified nation of loyal and patriotic citizens who lived together in peace and harmony for a very long time. No other ancient power had ever done that!

Why Study the Romans?

Our culture is founded upon many of the ideas and achievements of the Romans (including those they "borrowed" from the Greeks). Apart from their innovations in law and government, the Romans made substantial contributions to western civilization in the areas of engineering and architecture. The language of the Latins was spoken throughout the Roman empire, and it helped to bind the various peoples together. Modern Romance languages have evolved from Latin, and nearly one half of the words in English are derived from that ancient tongue. The Romans gave us the capital letters of our alphabet, the names of the months on our calendar, and, of course, Roman numerals.

Our everyday lives are influenced by all kinds of ideas and devices that date back to ancient Rome. For example, the Romans created the first hospitals, and they were the first to require the licensing of physicians and the inspection of food. They invented glass windowpanes, milestones, chemical fertilizer, theater curtains, scissors, ice cream, scales with weights, and the plane, brace and bit! And this is but a small part of their legacy!

The Divisions of Roman History

Roman civilization lasted for about one thousand years. Historians usually divide this rather long period into two major eras: the Republic (during which Rome expanded and gained control over the Italian peninsula) and the Empire (when a constitutional monarch based in Rome assumed power over the entire Mediterranean world). But it all started on those hills beside the Tiber, and so it is there that our story begins.

Questions:

1. How large was the Roman Empire?
2. Describe the geography of Italy.
3. Where is Latium?
4. How did the Latins get their name?
5. When was Rome founded?
6. What is the meaning of Mare Nostrum?
7. Name five contributions that the ancient Romans made to our modern culture.

Ideas to Think About:

1. Most historians arbitrarily use the birth of Christ as a convenient point in time for dating events. The letters "BC" stand for "before Christ" and refer to everything that happened until the moment of birth. Thus, the first one hundred years before the birth of Christ make up the first century BC (99-1 BC). The letters "AD" stand for *Anno Domini* (Latin for "the year of our Lord"), and they refer to everything that happened after the birth of Christ. The first one hundred years after the birth (AD 1-99) is the first century AD. Similarly, AD 100-199 is the second century AD, and so on. A key to remembering the century in relation to the actual date is this: The number of the century is always one more than the hundreds number of the date (1992 is in the twentieth century, while 191 is in

the second century). Remember, when citing time periods that are BC, you have to count backwards (for example, a person might have lived from 280 BC until 230 BC.

2. The earliest settlers of Italy raised sheep, goats, and pigs, but later on, herds of cattle were pastured in the river valleys and on the plains. Perhaps this explains why the word Italy (Italia) literally means "calf-land."

Projects:

1. Using this book and others in your classroom, draw a map of Italy. Indicate the following natural features: the Alps and the Apennine Mountains; the Po, Tiber, and Arno Rivers; the plains of Latium, Etruria, and Campania; Mount Vesuvius and Mount Etna; the Adriatic, Tyrrhenian, and Ionian Seas; Sicily, Corsica, and Sardinia. Label Rome in red letters. Make a map key to indicate mountains, plains, river valleys, and so on. Don't forget the compass rose.

2. The Indo-Europeans were nomads who wandered west from the steppes (plains) of modern Russia. They were the ancestors of many ancient peoples, including the Greeks and the Celts. Find out more about the Indo-Europeans and write a short report.

PART ONE — THE REPUBLIC

CHAPTER I — EARLY ROME

The Palatine Hill

The Latins first settled beside the Tiber River on the Palatine Hill. This lofty location provided them with an early warning of any approaching enemy, while the steep cliffs and the natural moat of marshes surrounding the hill offered some protection. They constructed small round houses out of poles (carved from tree branches) and turf. The design was a simple one. First they made holes in the rock and set the poles upright in them. (Recently, archaeologists have discovered some of these circles of holes cut into rock surfaces on the Palatine Hill.) Then they wove brush between the poles. This provided a sturdy frame for the house. They plastered the walls with clay derived from the river mud. Other long poles were used to construct a roof, which was thatched with bunches of grass.

fig. 3 — **A round house with thatched roof**

Each house had a small porch at its entrance.

The early Latins were simple farmers and shepherds. They grew wheat, barley, peas, and beans in the rich, volcanic soil of Latium, and they raised sheep and goats for their milk, skins, and meat. A few families even had pigs.

The Hilltop Villages

Gradually, new villages were established as farmers built their huts on the neighboring hilltops. Each village was ruled by a chieftain whose main duty was to defend his clansmen against invaders. When he was not engaged in battle, he tended his crops and animals just like everyone else. From earliest times, the family was a very strong social unit, the father controlling the lives of his wife and children.

The Burial Plots

The early settlers buried their dead in the marshy area between the Palatine and Capitoline hills. Archaeologists have discovered clay urns containing the ashes of cremated bodies there. The urns are shaped like the thatch-roofed huts we have just read about (this is how we know what those early dwellings looked like). The remains of

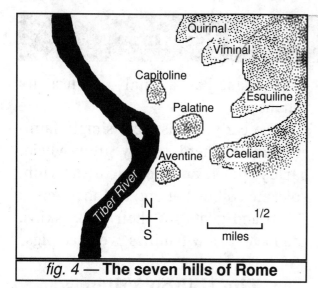

fig. 4 — **The seven hills of Rome**

bodies have also been found in the same burial grounds, and this suggests that neighboring communities held somewhat different religious beliefs concerning death.

Legends Describe the Founding of Rome

In later centuries, myths and legends were created that offered a more fanciful version of the founding of Rome. The most well known is a long epic (narrative poem) called THE AENEID. It was composed by the Roman poet Virgil in the first century BC. Virgil's story begins in the final days of the Trojan War (traditionally dated at about 1200 BC) when, after a siege of ten years, the Greeks enter the city of Troy and sack it. A Trojan prince named Aeneas manages to flee with his father and son. After many adventures, the trio ends up in Italy, where Aeneas marries the daughter of a local king and founds a dynasty of great rulers who will live in a city called Alba Longa. (The Tiber River was named after Tiberinus, one of the kings of Alba Longa.)

Another legend concerning the founding of Rome was passed down by word of mouth for generations until it was recorded by the Roman historian Livy (a contemporary of Virgil). This story begins when twin boys, Romulus and Remus, are born to Rhea Silva, daughter of King Numitor of Alba Longa (and descendant of Aeneas). Rhea claims that Mars, the Roman god of war, is the father of the boys. Soon after the birth, her wicked uncle Amulius deposes her father (Numitor) and orders a servant to drown the babies in the Tiber River. (Amulius wants to make sure that no one ever challenges his claim to the throne.) Fortunately, the servant takes pity on the babies and gently places them in a basket made of woven reeds, which then drifts downstream until it washes ashore beside a fig tree. The babies are soon found by a female wolf who has lost her cubs; she carries them to her den and nurtures them as if they were her own offspring. When they are about a year old, the boys are discovered by a local shepherd, and they spend the rest of their childhood living with him in his thatched hut on the Palatine Hill.

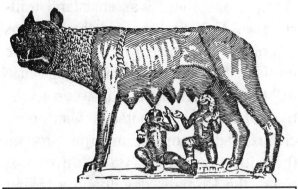

fig. 5 — **Statue of the she-wolf and the twins**

Romulus and Remus grow to be healthy and strong young men. When they learn of the circumstances of their birth, they return to Alba Longa, kill Amulius, and restore their grandfather Numitor to his throne. Then, planning to build themselves a city, they go to the place where the wolf had found them years before. They study the seven hills rising above the Tiber, but they cannot agree as to which hill should be the site of the city. Remus observes six vultures flying above the Aventine Hill, and, considering this sign to be a good omen, he sets out to build a city there. Romulus, however, sees twelve birds fly above the Palatine Hill, and so he decides to make that the site of his own city. (The Romans believed that the gods often revealed their wishes through the patterns in the flights of birds. This aspect of religion is called augury, and we will learn more about it later.)

Romulus yokes a white bull and a white cow to a plough and drives them in a circle around the top of the hill, marking the boundary of his city and casting up the dirt within the circle for the wall. Remus looks at the piles of dirt and then leaps over them, shouting, "This is what an enemy will do with your city wall!" Romulus immediately responds, "And this is what I shall do when he tries," as he slays his brother with a flint knife. Then, showing little remorse for this act of fratricide, Romulus returns to marking out his city, which he names Rome (after himself). He later becomes the city's first king. (According to tradition, Romulus laid out his city on April 21, 753 BC, and to this very day, April 21 is an important holiday in Italy.)

Of course, Romulus needs soldiers to defend his new city. He appeals to a number of vagrants living in the region and before long he has an army. When his men later complain that they have no wives, Romulus orders them to carry off the women belonging to the Sabines, a neighboring tribe. This, in turn, triggers a war with the Sabines, but (and this is surprising) the women end the fighting when they rush onto the battle-field and demand that their husbands, brothers and fathers lay down their arms. Not wishing to harm the women, the men agree to a truce, and they soon become allies rather than enemies. Already, the Romans have learned the value of resolving a conflict in a way that respects the rights of their former enemies.

Romulus rules wisely for thirty-seven years. Upon his death (according to legend he simply flies up to heaven during a thunderstorm), he predicts, "My Rome shall be the capital of the world!" As we shall see, he was right!

The Villages Merge

Whether we consider the historical evidence concerning the founding of Rome or the more fanciful legends, the fact remains that, in time, a cluster of hilltop villages came to dominate the eastern shores of the Tiber. The people living there were bound together by a common language and similar religions (based upon the worship of nature spirits). In the seventh century BC, the villages joined together in an annual religious festival called the Septimontium (meaning "Seven Hills"). This event encouraged the mingling of the various neighboring communities. By 600 BC, the villages had expanded and merged into a single large city, Rome.

The Advantages of Rome's Geographical Site

The geographic location of Rome had several advantages. First, the city overlooked the place where the Tiber was most easily crossed (the water was shallow and there was an island midstream). This site enabled the Romans to control the trade route between the northern territories and the south, since the foreign merchants had to cross the river at their very doorstep. Many merchants made Rome an important stop on their journeys, and as a result of this trade, the Romans developed a higher standard of living than that of other more isolated towns and villages in Latium.

Rome was also situated on the "salt road" (Via Salaria) along which bags of that useful mineral were transported from the salt flats at the mouth of the Tiber to inland regions. Salt was a highly prized commodity for preserving and flavoring foods.

Finally, by lying sixteen miles from

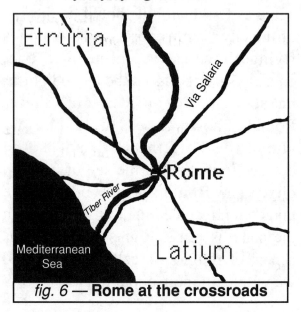

fig. 6 — **Rome at the crossroads**

the mouth of the river, Rome was near enough to the coast for its people to use the sea for fishing and transportation and yet far enough inland to be safe from marauding pirates. (It was difficult to navigate a vessel beyond the seven hills.) Eventually, the Romans would build a seaport city, Ostia.

The Etruscans

To the north of Latium lived a powerful people called the Etruscans. They inhabited about a dozen walled city-states in Etruria (modern Tuscany), a gently rolling land of fertile fields and rich natural resources lying between the Arno River and the Tiber. Not all historians agree about where the Etruscans came from. Many believe that they came to Italy by sea from Asia Minor in the eighth century BC; others feel that they migrated from the north. Such differing opinions make the study of ancient history all the more fascinating!

However they got there, once they had settled in Italy the Etruscans cleared the woodlands and drained the marshes in the region, thus creating many square miles of excellent farmland. They built underground tunnels to mine lead and copper, which they melted down to make tools and weapons. They also quarried marble and used the stone for statues and public buildings.

By the sixth century, the Etruscans had become a highly civilized people who enjoyed music, made beautiful pottery and statuettes, and designed delicate jewelry. They laid out their towns in orderly grid patterns, the wide cobblestone streets coming together at neat right angles.

Etruscan merchants and seamen dealt with many of the more prosperous peoples of the Mediterranean world, particularly the Greeks, with whom they exchanged new ideas and technologies. These commercial activities made the Etruscans extremely wealthy, and they soon enjoyed the comforts of a luxurious life style. Women occupied a high place in the Etruscan culture, and heredity was traced through the female line of the family. But although the Etruscans enjoyed the finer things of life, they were also formidable warriors.

The Greek Colonies

At about the same time that the Etruscans were becoming established in Etruria, a series of Greek colonies sprang up along the southeastern coast of Italy. The largest colonies were Cumae, which lay about three hundred miles south of Rome, and Tarentum (on the southeastern coast of Italy). Greeks also settled on the eastern part of Sicily, where Syracuse would one day become an important city. By the seventh century, the Greek colonists and the

Etruscans had become active trading partners.

fig. 7 — Etruria, Campania and the Greek colonies

Roman Culture Is Enriched By The Etruscans

The major city of the Etruscans was called Veii. It was only about twelve miles west of Rome, and so Etruscan merchants often made their way to Roman marketplaces. Eventually, powerful families from several Etruscan cities moved into the region of the seven hills, and by 600 BC they had gained control of Rome. They planned to use the Latin city as a base for further expansion into Campania.

By and large, the Etruscans had a positive impact on the development of Rome, for they helped to bring the rather backward Latin farmers into the mainstream of the more sophisticated peoples of the ancient world. Of key importance was their introduction of the Greek religion into Roman culture. The Greeks worshiped a pantheon of gods and goddesses who had human form and controlled all aspects of the natural world. It was the Greeks who first practiced augury (remember the vultures in the story of Romulus and Remus?), and they also tried to predict the future by divination (the examination of the entrails of sacrificed animals). These methods of determining the wishes of all-powerful gods and goddesses would play a significant role in the society of the Romans. We will learn more about them in Chapter V.

The Etruscans taught the Latin people how to mold metals for tools and weapons, and they encouraged the local craftsmen to seek broader markets for their products. They also introduced the concept of the arch and vault in the construction of buildings; we will learn how the Romans capitalized on these innovations. The Etruscans even established new fashion styles: The robes they wore would later be transformed into the familiar Roman toga!

Perhaps the greatest contribution of the Etruscans was their written alphabet (it was based upon one devised by the Greeks). Twenty-one of the Etruscan letters were adopted to record the Latin language; later, other sounds were given symbols, bringing the total number of letters to twenty-six. The Roman alphabet is the basis of the one we use today. The acquisition of writing enabled the Latin traders and craftsmen to keep records of their transactions, and it opened up all kinds of opportunities for communication among individuals.

The language of the Etruscans has yet to be deciphered; although nearly ten thousand fragments containing their ancient writing have been found, no one has been able to "crack the code."

Advances In Farming

The Etruscans taught the Romans a great deal about agriculture. Because the layer of volcanic soil of Latium is thin, the local farmers had been able to harvest only two crops in a field before having to move on to a new one. The Etruscans taught them to make better use of the soil.

Years earlier, the farmers in Etruria had noticed that crops planted in former pastures were unusually robust; they logically concluded that manure was a natural fertilizer, and from then on they customarily shoveled some onto their fields before each planting season. The Etruscan farmers also discovered that by rotating the kinds of crops that they planted in a given field they could prevent the soil from "wearing out." This is because each species takes a particular blend of nutrients from the earth. Therefore, they planted wheat one season, rye the next, oats the next, and finally clover or alfalfa (which they plowed into the dirt to enrich the soil). The next season the field was left fallow (unplanted). Once this cycle was completed, they started it all over again, confident that they would have a bountiful crop of wheat. These agricultural techniques (fertilization of the soil and rotation of crops) are standard practice for modern growers throughout the world, but for the humble farmers of Latium they were exciting and revolutionary procedures!

The Etruscans also taught the Latins how to dig drainage ditches in marshy areas to create new farmland and expand areas that could then be built upon. They even introduced the olives and grapes that were to become the staples of the Roman economy: Latin fields were planted with cuttings of olive trees and grape vines that grew in Etruria (these had originally been

fig. 8 — **A grapevine**

imported from Greece). Because the roots of olive trees and grape vines extend deep into the soil, these plants survived the heat and drought of the Italian summers, and produced rich harvests of olives and grapes in the fall.

The Roman Kings

Seven kings ruled Rome from 753 to 509 BC, beginning with the reign of Romulus. The kingship was not a hereditary one; rather, new leaders were chosen by the people. A king's duties were to lead the army (every citizen was expected to serve in the military), to judge major disputes, and to offer sacrifices to the gods. He was advised by the older (and presumably wiser) men of the community. These men were called the *patres familiarem* ("fathers of the families"), and as a group they were known as the Senate. (The word "senate" comes from the Latin *senex* which means "the old man"; "senile" also comes from this Latin term.) Besides the Senate, there was an assembly of ordinary townsmen called the Comitia Curiata which met to discuss such everyday matters as the fair price of grain.

A king named Numa Pompilius established the tradition of appointing priests to conduct local religious ceremonies. The pontifex maximus was the high priest who had authority over the others. From the beginning, the Roman priests were directly involved with the government and religious ceremonies were community affairs.

The last three kings of Rome were Etruscans: Tarquinius Priscus, Servius Tullius, and Tarquinius Superbus. They brought about important improvements in the city of Rome, including the building of the first wooden bridge across the Tiber and the construction of the great main sewer of the city (called the Cloaca Maxima, it is still in use today). They drained the marshy swamp that lay between the Palatine and Capitoline hills and paved it with flat stones. This reclaimed land would become the Roman Forum—a marketplace lined with public buildings and temples. The Etruscans built numerous roads as well as beautiful homes (for the rich) on the Palatine Hill. They improved the Circus Maximus (a huge race course) by constructing wooden stands around the track. Historically, Servius Tullius has been credited with putting up the first fortification around the seven hills (although some scholars say it was built later); known as the Servian Wall, it made Rome the largest enclosed area in Italy, and perhaps the world.

The Etruscans Are Driven From Rome

The last Etruscan king, Tarquinius Superbus (Tarquin the Proud), was haughty and cruel, but he did continue the tradition of city improvements. He oversaw the construction of a huge temple dedicated to Jupiter, Minerva and Juno on the Capitoline Hill. The temple was 210 feet long, and large terra-cotta (clay) statues of the three deities stood in the shrine within. Undoubtedly, one of the main purposes of this immense structure was to demonstrate the growing power of Rome. Before the temple was built, a bleeding head was found on the site. The Roman priests declared that this gruesome object was an omen that Rome would someday become "the head" of the world, but at the cost of war and bloodshed. We'll soon discover whether the priests were right!

In 509 BC the Latins revolted against their Etruscan masters and drove Tarquin out of Rome. The Senate then vehemently declared that they wanted no more kings. In fact, the word "king" was never again used in Roman politics. In place of the monarchy, the patres devised a new form of government in which the people themselves would play an important role.

Questions:

1. What were the geographic advantages of the Palatine Hill?
2. Who was Aeneas?
3. Why were the twin babies supposed to be drowned in the Tiber River?
4. When did Romulus found his city (the exact date)?
5. Where did the early Etruscans live?
6. What was the Etruscans' most important contribution to the culture of the early Romans?
7. Describe the government of early Rome.
8. Name three ways in which the Etruscan kings improved the city of Rome.
9. Who was the last Etruscan king to rule Rome?

Ideas To Think About:

1. After the Etruscans were driven out of Rome, they made several attempts to return to power. In about 500 BC, an Etruscan army marching toward Rome arrived at the foot of a wooden bridge that crossed the Tiber. As they moved onto the bridge, Horatius Cocles, the Roman army captain charged with defending it, dashed forward and bravely faced the enemy soldiers. He ordered the two soldiers with him to cut down the bridge behind him while he held off the Etruscans with his sword. He

stood his ground until the bridge behind him had been destroyed; then he plunged, in full armor, into the waters of the Tiber and (in one version) swam to shore. Horatius became a model of Roman courage and loyalty. He was the first man to be honored by his city with a statue in the Forum. His great sense of patriotism is reflected in the following lines of the poem "Horatius" by the English poet Macaulay:

"Then out spake brave Horatius,
The Captain of the Gate;
"To every man upon this earth
Death cometh soon or late,
And how can man die better
Than facing fearful odds,
For the ashes of his fathers
And the temples of his gods!"

2. A Roman leader named Lucius Junius Brutus was the subject of another famous legend. After Tarquin was driven out of Rome, the sons of Brutus became involved in a political plot to restore the power of the Etruscan king. The plot was discovered and the brothers were brought to trial. It was Brutus' painful duty not only to pronounce his sons guilty of treason against the state but to sentence them to death. Like Horatius, the loyal and patriotic Brutus became a Roman hero.

3. The Romans frequently went to war over the ownership of land. In yet another legend, Rome was drawn into conflict with the city of Alba Longa. In order to avoid needless bloodshed, the two cities agreed that three brothers on each side would fight (instead of the armies). The Roman Horatii were chosen to fight the Curiatii of Alba. Soon after the fighting began, two Horatii were killed and three Curiatii were wounded. The surviving Roman brother pretended to flee, but then he ambushed and killed each of the Curiatii as they pursued him. As in the legend of Horatius at the bridge, courage and tenacity won out despite great odds. One of the Curiatti was engaged to the sister of Horatius; when she mourned her dead lover, Horatius killed her, too (for her lack of patriotism!).

4. Most of what we know about the way of life of the Etruscans derives from their way of death. This is because they built large underground tombs for their dead. They decorated the walls with paintings depicting everyday situations, and they placed near the bodies weapons, tools, and works of art, most likely for use in "the next life." Terracotta coffins shaped like dining couches have been discovered in some of the tombs; in many cases, the figures of a husband and wife recline together on the funerary couch. They seem to be anticipating the meal that they will enjoy together for eternity.

5. The fasces, an ax tied to a bundle of sticks by leather thongs, was the official symbol of an Etruscan king. It signified the king's power to beat and behead his rebellious subjects! The fasces was later adopted by the Romans as the symbol of their highest ranking government leader. Special attendants called lictors carried the fasces in ceremonial parades. In the twentieth century, the fasces was adopted once again, this time by the Italian leader Benito Mussolini, and from it was derived the name of his political philosophy—Fascism.

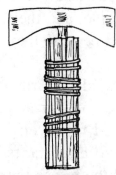

fig. 9 — **The fasces**

6. Some people believe that the name of Rome is actually derived from the Greek word "rhome" which means "brute force."

Projects:

1. On his way to Italy, Aeneas shared a romantic interlude with Queen Dido of Carthage. Read about this famous story, and present a report to your class.

2. Clearly, the Romans owed a tremendous amount to the Etruscans. Why, then, did they rebel against their rule? Find out more about the reign of Tarquin the Proud. Write a short paper offering your explanation for the Roman eviction of the Etruscans.

3. "The Oath of the Horatii" is a famous painting by the nineteenth century French artist David. (Reread #3 in "Ideas To Think About" above.) Find a picture of the painting in an art book in your library. Study the picture carefully, and then write a paragraph describing (in detail) the dramatic moment that the artist has tried to depict.

4. Find out about the legend of Gaius Mucius Scaevola, the Roman soldier who held his right hand in a flame without flinching. What did he expect to prove by inflicting his body to such pain?

CHAPTER II — The Republican Form of Government

A New Concept of Leadership

The patres who gathered together after Tarquin was driven out of Rome were determined to create a new form of government that was responsive to the needs of the Latin people. They had had enough of kings who ruled according to their personal whims. What was needed was a system that enabled the people to choose the men who would lead them and also offered them a say in the decision-making process. The new government that gradually evolved to meet these needs was called the Republic, a name derived from the Latin words *res publica* which mean "the public thing." The Roman Republic was conceived in 509 BC. and it lasted over four hundred years.

From the start, the abuses so often connected with monarchy were avoided by placing at the head of the government not one but two men. These leaders were called consuls and they served a one-year term. The patres reasoned that by sharing the job, each consul would watch the other and neither could claim absolute power. As the word "consul" suggests, the two men were expected to consult each other about major decisions; compromise was a necessary goal, since each had the power to negate the acts of the other. This arrangement could have resulted in disaster if the two consuls couldn't get along. However, the Romans were flexible people, and their government worked in part because they passionately wanted it to!

The consuls commanded the army and decided upon policies of war and peace. They were escorted to government meetings by twelve attendants called lictors who carried the fasces (an ax tied to a bundle of rods symbolizing power—see page 19). The first two men elected to the position of consul were named Brutus (see page 18) and Collatinus. Every January first, two new consuls were sworn in. On this occasion, bulls were sacrificed to the god Jupiter to thank him for his protection in the last year (and in hopes that it would continue for the coming twelve months).

Often, in spite of all good intentions, the dual command became cumbersome, and so the Romans restructured the system so that each consul presided as chief executive on alternate days; in times of war, the same arrangement applied on the battlefield. Should both consuls be incapacitated in wartime, a single military leader (called a Dictator) would be appointed to lead the army for a period of six months, after which time he would relinquish his power.

The Role of the Senate

The Senate continued to be an important part of the government, now serving as a body of advisors to the consuls. Senators served for life. They elected the consuls from among their own ranks. Former consuls automatically became senators again, and so over the years the Senate evolved into a group of highly experienced and knowledgeable statesmen.

Three hundred senators served at one time. Apart from advising the consuls, they debated issues affecting the public interest and then voted on possible solutions. Their decisions were not binding, but they provided the basis for future laws. The Senate met in the Curia, a building in the Roman Forum.

What kind of men served in the Senate? At the start, they were all patricians, men from the oldest and most important families (they were called patricians because they were descended from the original patres familiarem.) The patricians were organized into clans, the names of which generally ended in -ius (such as Lucius, Cornelius or Fabius). Today the word "patrician" is used to describe someone who comes from an old and wealthy family.

The Assembly

The Assembly (*Comitia Centuriata*) was a gathering of Roman citizens that met on an open plain called the Field of Mars (*Campus Martius*); they were summoned by a trumpet call when the consuls thought fit. The Comitia Centuriata replaced the Comitia Curiata of Etruscan days. It had three main functions: to vote on laws after proposals had been made by the Senate, to make sure the laws were kept, and to elect magistrates (government officials). In times of crisis, they voted whether or not Rome should go to war. For many years, the Assembly members spent most of their time listening to the campaign speeches of hopeful candidates. In 287 BC, however, they were granted the power to initiate and then enact laws (subject, of course, to the approval of the Senate).

The Plight of the Plebeians

The Roman Republic was hardly democratic. The consuls, senators, and even most Assembly members were patricians. This is partly because only the patricians had the money necessary to get elected to public office; furthermore, only they could afford to devote great chunks of time to government meetings, for which there was no pay. Such rule by an elite group of people is called an aristocracy, a Greek word meaning "rule by the select few." Yet, the ordinary people, known as the plebeians, outnumbered the patricians nine to one! The plebeians suspected, (and rightly so), that the patricians made many decisions to suit their own special interests, and so they began to protest the fact that they had no voice in the government. In 494 BC they staged a general strike and threatened to leave Rome and build their own city somewhere else! The patricians needed the plebeians because they made up a large part of the Roman army, and so they reluctantly gave in to their demands.

The organization of the central government was then revised so that the plebeians could elect two officials from their own ranks to represent their interests and protect their rights. These officials were called tribunes, and although they could not make laws, they could defeat them. Simply by saying *veto* (a Latin word meaning "I forbid"), a tribune could prevent passage of those proposals made by the Senate and the consuls that he felt ran counter to the needs of the common people. Even-

tually there were ten tribunes.

The *Concilium Plebis* was established soon afterwards. This plebeian assembly (from which patricians were excluded) was empowered to pass decrees (called plebiscites), which affected the entire city. Over the years, the plebeians gained admission to virtually all public offices. In 366 BC a plebeian became consul, and from then on it was customary for one of the two consuls to be a member of that humbler class. Yet, despite these advances in the power of the plebeians, the patricians continued to dominate the Roman government.

The Political Ladder of Success

There was a hierarchy of government positions. In fact, an ambitious young man with the right social credentials could devote much of his adult life to advancing from one political office to another until he reached the pinnacle of success. Starting his career at the age of thirty, he could be elected quaestor (a city treasurer). Then on to the office of aedile (supervisor of the city's food supply, traffic, and entertainment). At the age of thirty-nine, an experienced magistrate could be elected a praetor (one of eight judges who presided over the law courts). An ex-praetor was right in line to become consul, followed by "retirement" to the Senate, where he could spend the rest of his years as a highly respected elder of Roman politics.

Once every five years, two censors were elected. Their duties were to arrange the names of the population on large charts according to their wealth for the purposes of taxation, army service, and position in the Assembly. They also rooted out unworthy citizens (men convicted of crimes or accused of disloyalty), and it is from this function that our modern word "censorship" is derived.

The office of pontifex maximus was retained from Etruscan times. The man who held this position was in charge of virtually all religious activities in Rome, and he wielded considerable power and influence.

two consuls

| 300 senators | 10 tribunes |

citizen assemblies

| questors, aediles, praetors, censors, priests |

fig. 10 — **Divisions of power in the Republican government**

The Roman Code of Laws

The legal system that evolved during the Republic is one of Rome's greatest contributions to modern civilization. At first, Roman law was little more than a collection of traditional beliefs, and, during the first years of the Republic, the patrician magistrates tended to pick and choose among the decisions of the past to resolve a conflict. The plebeians worried (for good reason) that they were at a disadvantage in legal disputes, and in 450 BC their assembly issued a plebiscite requiring that all laws be written down. They hoped that in this way they could establish a permanent standard of decisions and punishments that would apply to people of both social classes.

This plebiscite resulted in the first Roman code of law. It was called the Twelve Tables (or Tablets), because the laws were written on twelve bronze tablets that were posted in the Forum. The code was a kind of bill of rights, and it established a precedent whereby all legal disputes had to be judged according to the same set of rules.

Some of the laws posted on the tablets were very harsh. For example, a burglar who was caught in the act could be killed on the spot. If a man broke another's leg and didn't pay for damages, he lost his own leg. If someone composed a song which brought dishon-

or to another person, he was clubbed to death. And anyone caught stealing crops at night was beaten with rods. Yet, the codification of the laws led to greater justice since there was now a common basis for judging all disputes.

Henceforth, a person accused of a crime had the right to face and question his accusers, and the judges treated all people equally, regardless of social class. Every case was recorded, so that in future disputes the judges could draw upon the decisions previously made in similar circumstances. Of critical importance in the Roman concept of justice was the presumption that a person was innocent until or unless he was proven guilty. This premise, which we take for granted in our modern society, was a revolutionary concept in the ancient world. Traditionally, it had been the other way around!

The praetors judged cases in law courts called basilica, which were located near the Forum. Gradually a complex set of laws evolved as new decisions were added to those listed on the Twelve Tables. Changes in the established laws were rare, however, and they had to be agreed to by the Senate, Assembly and tribunes.

The Army

There were no full-time soldiers in the early Republic. When neighboring tribes invaded Roman soil, the consuls summoned all the able-bodied men. These soldier-farmers left their plows, took up their weapons, and proudly marched off to battle. Afterwards, their duty done, they returned to their fields. The early Romans considered the ability to work hard and to fight bravely among the greatest of manly virtues.

A citizen named Lucius Quinctius Cincinnatus became the model for all Romans of the period. In 458 BC Rome was at war with a neighboring nation. A consul had been captured, and the army needed a gifted leader. But who? Cincinnatus was an ex-consul who had retired to a small farm outside the city. His bravery and patriotism were well known. And so, as Cincinnatus was plowing his field, he was approached by a group of senators who asked him to become Rome's Dictator and to rescue the consul. Cincinnatus accepted the appointment without a second thought. He led the Roman army to victory and liberated the captured consul in only sixteen days! Then, his duty done, he returned to his plow. He expected no praise or reward, for he put his duty to Rome before any consideration of personal gain. He exemplified what the Romans called *gravitas*, a devout loyalty to the spirit of public service. The story of Cincinnatus was told to generations of young Romans. He remains a legendary hero, and the city of Cincinnati, Ohio is named for him.

Questions:

1. What does the word "republic" mean in Latin?
2. Why were there two consuls at one time?
3. Describe the Senate.
4. What were the duties of the Assembly?
5. Who were the patricians and the plebeians?
6. What does the word "veto" mean in Latin?
7. What is a plebiscite?
8. Describe the "ladder to success" in Roman politics.
9. What were the Twelve Tablets?
10. Why was it important to have a written code of laws?

Ideas to Think About

1. The speaker's platform in the Forum was decorated with the prows of ships that had been captured by the Romans in the third century BC. The Latin word for prow is *rostrum*, and even today the speaker's platform in an assembly hall is called a rostrum.

2. The Comitia Centuriata was divided into 193 groups that were based on wealth. In theory, each group had one hundred men, but in practice it turned out otherwise. Each citizen who could provide his own armor, spear, shield and sword was assigned to a voting unit of one hundred men (this unit of men having one vote in the Comitia). Poorer citizens who couldn't afford as many weapons were assigned to more numerous units (more than one hundred men but still one vote). Wealthy men with horses were put in units of less than one hundred (still allotted one vote). Therefore, the voting favored the wealthiest men, who had a lot of power despite their fewer numbers. Also, the more prestigious groups voted first, and the majority won. There were frequent occasions when a low-ranking group didn't have a chance to vote at all, since voting was stopped as soon as a majority was reached.

3. The Greek historian Polybius (203-120 BC) lived for many years in Rome. He wrote about the Roman government of his time in glowing terms, and he praised the system of checks and balances that supposedly prevented an abuse of power. In the eighteenth century AD, the French political theorist Montesquieu used Polybius' book as the basis of his own theory of the separation of powers (his work is called THE SPIRIT OF THE LAWS). Our founding fathers (Adams, Madison, Jefferson, etc.) in turn used Montesquieu's work as the basis for their drafting of the US Constitution with its system of checks and balances among the legislative, executive, and judicial branches of government.

4. The Twelve Tables forbade the intermarriage of patricians and plebeians, thus widening the gap between the two social groups. This restriction was removed in the later years of the Republic.

Projects:

1. On poster board make a chart showing the three branches of the modern American government—the executive, the legislative, and the judicial. Then indicate the governing bodies of the Roman Republic from which each branch might have evolved.

2. The Romans got many of their political ideas from the Greeks. Find out about the democracy that flourished in Athens in the fifth century AD. Write a short paper explaining how many of the Greek concepts were reflected in the design of the government of the Roman Republic.

3. In later years, a rule was made establishing forty-two as the minimum age for a consul. What is the minimum age for a candidate for the US presidency? Who was the youngest president? Who was the oldest?

4. Some patrician families could boast of having produced several consuls. A new consul coming from such a family was called a *nobilis* (noble), while someone who was the first in his family to achieve the highest office was called a *novus homo* (new man). As you might expect, the new men were looked down upon by the nobles and had to prove their worthiness! Can you think of examples of similar behavior in modern times?

CHAPTER III — ROME BEGINS TO EXPAND

The Latin League

The Romans did not set out to aggressively expand their territory at the expense of neighboring tribes. However, squabbles over land ownership did frequently erupt into large-sale fighting. During the first one hundred years of the Republic, Roman soldiers came to blows with nearby hillsmen nearly every summer. At these times, they fought with such courage and determination that they usually won.

As Rome gradually increased in size, the other towns of Latium became very nervous. They formed an organization called the Latin League, whose main purpose was to defend their plain against the tribes living in the surrounding hills, but they also hoped to prevent Rome's domination of the entire region. However, when the hillsmen seemed to present a greater threat than the Romans, a peace treaty was negotiated in which Rome became the leader of the League. All the Latin cities agreed to help each other in the event of invasion and to share the booty of any successful battle.

The End of Etruscan Power

Since the exile of Tarquin the Proud, the Etruscans had been commercial as well as military rivals of the Romans. This situation was altered in 396 BC, when Roman soldiers captured and destroyed the Etruscan city of Veii after a siege of several years. The winning general of this long and bitter struggle was Marcus FURIUS Camillus!

The Gauls

The Roman soldiers were not always victorious, however. Soon after the fall of Veii, the army's attention was suddenly drawn to a band of fierce and blood-thirsty warriors called the Gauls (a tribe of Celts). These uncivilized nomads from central Europe had moved into the Po valley, and they were launching a series of raids in the northern Italian countryside. The Gauls were formidable long-haired giants; they screamed deafening war cries and then leapt at their startled opponents, brandishing their great iron swords!

In 390 BC the Roman army marched north and bravely faced the Gauls at the Allia River. However, the highly disciplined Roman soldiers were no match for the wild-eyed barbarians, who easily slashed through their lines and then proceeded on to sack the city of Rome. This was the only time that Rome ever fell to an invading army (until its final defeat in the fifth century AD). And yet, not all of Rome was captured by the Gauls. A small detachment of Roman soldiers held out for days, perched above the steep cliff of the Capitoline Hill (where most of the temples were located). One moonlit night, a group of enemy warriors began to scale the cliff. As the first man reached the top, he startled the sacred geese of Juno that lived near the goddess' temple. The noisy cackling of the birds awoke Marcus Manlius, the Roman captain of the guard. He raced to where the Gaul had just gotten a foot-hold on the crest of the hill and struck him hard with his shield. The warrior fell back and tumbled down the cliff, knocking off the men who had been climbing behind him. Those who managed to scramble to the top were slain by Manlius and the soldiers who had now joined him. The Gauls never captured the Capitoline Hill, and the courage of Manlius was remembered by future generations of Romans.

fig. 11 — *Sacred geese*

The Gauls remained in Rome for some time, however, until the Romans finally managed to bribe them to leave with a payment of about one thousand pounds of gold. Their occupation was a great humiliation that the Romans never forgot. (In fact, July 18—the day the Gauls sacked the city—was observed as a time of mourning in Rome for centuries.) The invaders withdrew to the Po River Valley and settled there. They continued to raid the local region from time to time, but they never again threatened Rome.

Just to be on the safe side, however, the Romans replaced the old Servian Wall with a more substantial barrier. A new wall made of volcanic stone extended for five and one half miles and enclosed an area of more than a thousand acres.

A New Army Formation

The bitter experience with the Gauls had an important effect upon the military tactics of the Roman army. Since the days when there were still kings, Roman soldiers had marched into battle in a phalanx, a tight and inflexible military formation invented by the Greeks. Each soldier carried a shield and a long thrusting spear. The entire unit moved as one man, and its success depended upon its ability to push through the front line of the enemy army.

Camillus (the very same M. Furius Camillus who destroyed Veii) was appointed Dictator after the Gallic invasion. He had observed to his horror how easily the freely wielded swords of the Gauls cut through the rigid Roman phalanx. Many of the barbarians simply ducked under the Roman shields and slashed their opponents in the stomach! Camillus concluded that his men could fight more effectively if they were divided into smaller groups that could turn and move independently. Furthermore, he believed that the traditional thrusting spears should be replaced with javelins and swords. His ideas eventually led to a reorganization that would make the Roman army the most invincible force in the ancient world. We will study military matters in greater detail in Chapter VIII.

Victory over the Samnites

The Samnites were a tribe of hill people living southeast of Rome. They claimed ownership of the plain of Campania, the pleasant fertile region that also appealed to the Latin farmers. Inevitably, war broke out. The Romans lost the first phase of the Samnite Wars in 321 BC, when their army of about ten thousand men (led by both consuls) was forced to surrender at the Caudine Fork near Capua. It was this disaster that convinced the Roman generals to act

upon the proposals of Camillus and transform their battle formation.

At about the same time, a wide paved road known as the Appian Way was completed. It stretched southward from Rome and enabled the army to send soldiers and supplies to Campania at an impressive speed.

Meanwhile, the Samnites allied themselves with groups of Etruscans, Sabines and Gauls; their combined numbers seemed to promise an easy victory. But after a number of small battles, the Romans finally crushed their adversaries at Sentinum (in 295 BC). This battle did not go well for the Romans until Publius Decius Mus (the consul in command) inspired his men by courageously charging through the enemy line. He was killed, but his sacrifice kindled among his soldiers the determination to plunge into the fray and on to victory. According to one story, omens had predicted that the

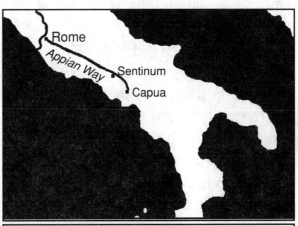

fig. 12 — **The region of Samnite Wars**

winning side would be the one whose leader was killed; this might help to explain Mus' suicidal dash into the spears of his opponents! In the end, Rome was master of Campania as well as Latium.

Old Enemies Become Allies of Rome

The Romans treated their vanquished enemies with respect, allowing them to retain their local government, customs, and religious traditions. However, every conquered city and town was required to adopt the foreign policy of Rome and send men to serve in the Roman army. When they had proved their loyalty to Rome, the once hostile Italian tribesmen could become Roman citizens. Thus, former adversaries were eased into Roman society, and the status of citizenship became a much sought-after prize among those who had previously opposed the dominance of the city on the Tiber.

Roman Colonies

Rome's population was rapidly growing. For the time being, settlement in the newly acquired land in Latium and Campania helped to remedy the increasingly crowded living conditions in and around the city. Villages were established at strategic crossroads in the region south of Rome, and free land was offered to those citizens who wished to live there. Among the first to take advantage of this offer were the soldiers themselves, who had observed the beautiful, rolling landscapes while marching into battle. Once the fighting was over, they settled down and began farming on the fertile plains. A small colony at Ostia (at the mouth of the Tiber) would later grow into Rome's major shipping port.

The Pyrrhic Wars

By 282 BC, the Romans controlled most of Italy from the Po Valley southward to the cluster of Greek trading colonies referred to as Magna Graecia. Tarentum was now a thriving commercial center on the eastern coast of Italy. Although the Greek city had signed a treaty with Rome that guaranteed its control of the local offshore waters, its citizens were uneasy about the growing power of Rome. So when a fleet of Roman ships disregarded the treaty and entered the offshore waters, the Tarentines sank them! When Rome declared war, the people of Tarentum realized that they had "bitten off more than they could chew," and so they quickly dispatched a messenger to King Pyrrhus of Epirus in northern Greece asking for help. Pyrrhus was an ambitious military leader, and, seeing an opportunity to gain control of southern

Italy, he immediately set sail with twenty-five thousand mercenaries (hired soldiers) and twenty war elephants.

This invasion marked the Romans' first encounter with troops (and elephants!) from overseas. As the armies took their positions on the battlefield, Pyrrhus's army lined up in the rigid phalanx formation: His solid line of soldiers carried massive sixteen-foot spears that protruded from the first rank like the quills of a giant porcupine. On the wings waited the cavalry and the elephants. The Romans, thanks to the innovations of Camillus, formed three lines rather than one, and each line was made up of smaller units called maniples.

The Romans should have had the advantage. But although the infantry could maneuver more easily than the awkward and unwieldy phalanx, the cavalry was poorly trained. The Romans were never enthusiastic horsemen; in fact, it was not unusual for a rider to dismount his horse and join in the hand-to-hand fighting with the other soldiers! Now, as Pyrrhus's army moved forward, the Roman horses panicked at the strange smell of the elephants, wheeled around, and galloped though the startled ranks of Roman footsoldiers. Their riders could not control them! Pyrrhus immediately took advantage of the confusion and charged ahead. The

Romans fought valiantly, however, and the battle ended with no clear winning side. Pyrrhus lost a huge number of soldiers. A second encounter at Asculum proved equally bloody; although the Greeks claimed victory, the outcome was again indecisive. According to legend, Pyrrhus pondered the great numbers of dead Greek soldiers and remarked, "One more victory like this and we are lost!" Today a Pyrrhic victory is something won at a very great cost.

Pyrrhus marched to within forty miles of Rome, but the Roman soldiers prevented him from advancing further. After a long and discouraging series of skirmishes, Pyrrhus finally asked for peace terms. The Romans refused, saying that they didn't make peace with invaders!

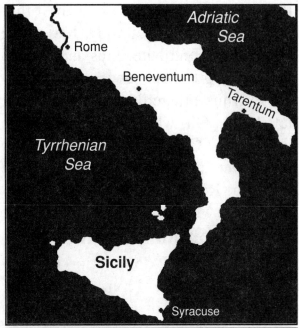

fig. 13 — **Battlesites of the Pyrrhic Wars**

Pyrrhus then moved on to Sicily where he drove the Carthaginians from the Greek colony of Syracuse. Once again his victory cost many lives, and when he returned to Italy in 275 BC, he had only one third of his original army. By this time, the Romans had had time to rethink their strategy. As the two armies marched towards each other at Beneventum, the Roman troops hurled their javelins directly at the elephants, causing the startled beasts to stampede and trample the Greek footsoldiers. A few ingenius Romans even mounted stoves on chariots and threw hot coals at the fleeing elephants! Although the outcome of this battle was (as usual) inconclusive, the Romans claimed victory and Pyrrhus withdrew to Epirus. The Greek cities became part of the Roman territory, but unlike the other conquered regions of Italy, they were required to contribute ships and men to the fledgling Roman navy.

Pyrrhus allegedly remarked as he left Italy, "Oh, what a battlefield I am leaving for Carthage and Rome!" His words were prophetic ones, for Carthage was to be Rome's next adversary.

Rome Commands All of Italy

The Romans' domination of Italy was now complete. From the Po River Valley to the tip of Italy's "toe," they commanded over fifty-two thousand square miles of land and nearly three million people. In the process, Rome had become the dominant power in the Mediterranean community.

Questions:

1. What was the Latin League?
2. Why did the Romans treat the people they defeated so well?
3. Who were the Gauls?
4. How did the sacred geese save the city of Rome?
5. How did Camillus reform the army?
6. What was the Appian Way?
7. How did the Roman colonies strengthen the feelings of patriotism?
8. Describe the Roman cavalry.
9. What is a Pyrrhic victory?

Ideas to Think About

1. When the Gauls invaded Rome, they found that many of the able-bodied citizens had fled. But the more aged senators had refused to flee; dressed in their ceremonial robes and seated upon ivory-inlaid thrones in the Forum, they calmly awaited the onslaught of the barbarians. As they burst upon the scene, the Gauls suddenly stopped and stared in amazement at the unmoving old gentlemen. Then Brennus, the Gallic chieftain, stroked the beard of Senator Marcus Papirius to see if he was indeed alive; when the Roman struck back with his ivory staff, Brennus drew his sword

and slew the senator on the spot. What followed was a massacre of the Roman elders. This story was often told in ancient Rome. The stoic senators symbolized the Roman ideal of facing an inevitable death with dignity and calm.

2. The Romans loved the order of a perfect square. The farmers' fields were always square, and there was a practical reason for this: since a wooden plowshare hardly scratched the surface of the hard, dry earth, the farmer had to plow a second time at right angles to the first in order to prepare the soil for cultivation. The Romans also built square cities, square houses, square temples, and square army barracks. Augurers (see page 11) even divided the sky into imaginary squares, and told the future by noting in which squares birds appeared!

3. The Gauls were headhunters. After a battle, they often cut off the heads of their enemies and displayed them in their villages.

4. As we have seen, the early Romans were gifted in political and military organization. Yet, literature, art, and philosophy were almost unknown in early Republican times.

Projects

1. Learn more about the Greek phalanx and write a short report. A good source of information is THE GREEK ARMY by Peter Connolly.

2. Draw a picture of a Gaul. Consult the books in your room. Then, use your imagination!

3. The Romans encountered war elephants for the first time when Pyrrhus invaded Italy. They were to encounter them many times again. Alexander the Great learned about these gentle behemoths when he marched into India. Find out more about the history of war elephants, and write a short report.

4. Give three modern examples of a Pyrrhic victory. They can come from your own personal experiences or from your knowledge of current events.

CHAPTER IV — THE PUNIC WARS

Carthage

Across the Mediterranean Sea in North Africa lay the prosperous trading port of Carthage. It had been settled hundreds of years earlier by colonists from Tyre, a city in Phoenicia (modern Lebanon). In the Phoenician language, the city's name was *Kart-hadast* (meaning "New Town"). Carthage became an independent nation soon after its founding, and by the third century BC it had acquired a rich commercial empire that extended over much of northern Africa, the islands of Sardinia and Corsica, and parts of Sicily and Spain.

Indeed, Carthage controlled the western Mediterranean world as well as the lives of three million people.

The merchants of Carthage were mainly interested in trading metals—gold, silver and tin. Gold and silver, of course, were used to make jewelry and other luxury items, but tin was required for more practical purposes. It could be melted down with copper to produce bronze and then molded into a variety of useful items, ranging from weapons to pots and pans. Bronze was preferable to copper because it was a much harder metal. Carthaginian ships were even

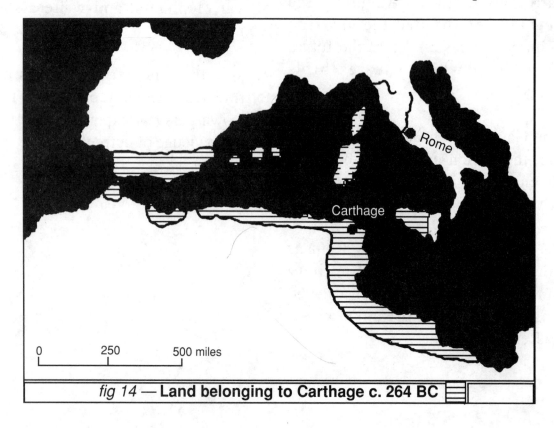

fig 14 — **Land belonging to Carthage c. 264 BC**

known to venture into the stormy Atlantic to obtain cargoes of tin from Britain. Such a voyage required great courage, for in those early times Britain was believed to lie at the very edge of the world!

An Invincible Navy

Carthage was situated on a high promontory overlooking the sea. The city was surrounded by three huge walls whose long expanse was broken at intervals by high look-out towers. Even the harbor was protected by a ring of stone barriers. Not that the Carthaginians were interested in war; when they occasionally acquired new territory, it was for purposes of improving their commercial network. But they were very concerned about the defense of their ports and merchant ships, so they built a powerful fleet of bronze-prowed vessels. In a very short time, the Carthaginian navy virtually eliminated pirates from the western Mediterranean.

Carthage also had an army. Its soldiers were mostly mercenaries (hired fighters from other nations). The generals remained with the army from year to year, unlike the Roman leaders who had to return to Rome annually for elections. However, when people of the Mediterranean world talked about the military might of Carthage, they were referring to the navy, not the army.

War Breaks Out In Sicily

When the Romans completed their conquest of Italy, Carthage controlled half of Sicily and showed signs of taking over the entire island. The Romans coveted the island because it's fertile soil produced a bountiful harvest of grain. At the same time, Sicily lay almost mid-way between Europe and Africa, its eastern shore only five miles from the Italian coast, and the Romans must have felt uneasy about such a strategic site falling completely into the hands of the huge Carthaginian Empire. So when the Sicilian city of Messina revolted against Carthage and asked for aid, Rome responded aggressively. The skirmish that followed provided the excuse for a declaration of war against Carthage.

Thus began the first of the three Punic Wars between Rome and Carthage. (Punic is the Latin word for Phoenician.) For over sixty years, the two super powers of the Mediterranean world would vie with one another, the long bouts of fighting to be interrupted only twice by negotiated peace settlements. The three wars cost Rome half a million men.

A New Kind of Warship

Once war had been declared, the Romans found themselves in a predicament. Although their army was a mighty force, it was of little use against a strong naval power like Carthage. It was a curious situation: Carthage had a great fleet but no significant army, while Rome had a fine army but no fleet! Clearly something had to be done, so the Romans put their heads together and came up with a practical solution. The first step was to construct a fleet of ships as swift as those of Carthage. By a convenient twist of fate, a Carthaginian warship had run aground on the coast of Latium, and it became the perfect model for the vessels of the new Roman navy!

Whole forests were quickly cut down for their timber, and a fleet of 140 Roman galley ships was built in the incredibly short time of 60 days. Each ship was 120 feet long and 14 feet wide, with five banks of oars and a battering ram at the prow. It carried 300 sailors (soldiers manning the oars) and, when not directly engaged in warfare, it carried 40 marines (fighting men). During a battle the number of marines was increased to 120.

Since the Roman soldiers had no sailing experience, they practiced rowing on large wooden stages erected on the land. This must have been an amusing sight! But even a new fleet of ships and enthusiastic crews did not put the Romans on an equal footing with the invincible Carthaginian navy that had dominated the seas for over a century.

The Romans needed some kind of advantage. They knew that they excelled at hand-to-hand combat, but how could they turn a sea fight into a land battle? They solved this dilemma with a very practical invention: a hinged gangplank with a sharp iron spike at the end. It was called the *corvus* (Latin for "the raven") because its spiked end resembled the beak of a bird. When not in use, the corvus could be raised and tied to a mast with ropes; when needed, it was swivelled around and lowered over the side of the ship.

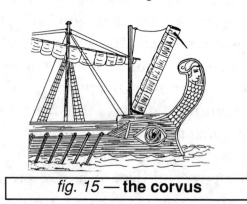

fig. 15 — **the corvus**

Once this ingenious device had been installed on each of the ships, the Romans were ready to try out their truly unique naval strategy. This is how it worked. First, a ship had to avoid being rammed by a Carthaginian vessel and maneuver into position along side it. Then the marines on board hurled javelins at the enemy seamen while other crewmen locked the two ships together with iron hooks attached to long ropes. Quickly the corvus was swivelled into position, and as it dropped down, the spike sank into the deck of the enemy ship. Now the Roman soldiers could dash across the gangplank and fight the Carthaginians as they would have on a field of battle!

The First Punic War

The first Punic War began in 264 BC and it lasted for twenty-three years. The Roman's naval strategy usually worked, and it won them many battles. However, the inexperienced crews had difficulty maneuvering their ships in bad weather, and on more than one occasion nearly the entire fleet was sunk. But at such times, the determined Romans simply built more battleships and resumed the fighting. In the end, they were victorious. In fact, the final battle of the first Punic War was fought without the corvus: The Romans defeated the Carthaginians in a conventional naval battle. That says a lot for the adaptability of the Roman soldier!

This was the first war the Romans fought beyond the borders of Italy, and it was a costly one. Over one hundred thousand Roman soldiers died and five hundred warships were destroyed (mostly in storms). Nonetheless, Rome had challenged the mightiest power in the western Mediterranean and won. This was certainly a consolation! In the peace settlement, Carthage was ordered to abandon Sicily and to pay a huge sum of money. The island became Rome's first foreign province. (The Romans later seized Corsica and Sardinia as well.) Unlike the Italian allies, the people of the provinces had to surrender their land and pay tribute to Rome (usually one tenth of their wheat harvest).

Carthage Looks To Spain

Now that the fighting was over, Carthage looked for ways to rebuild her empire. Hamilcar Barca, a much respected Carthaginian general who had fought Sicily, led an army to Spain. Carthage had established trading posts there years earlier, and Hamilcar now hoped to conquer that primitive country, which was so rich in natural resources (especially gold and silver). He also planned to recruit many of the spirited young Spaniards into his army.

Hannibal Enters the Scene

Hamilcar's eldest son was named Hannibal. At the age of nine, the boy had made a pledge to his father that he would fight the Romans until he defeated them. He was well educated, and he learned to speak Greek fluently. As a young man, Hannibal helped his father conquer most of Spain. He was a fearless fighter, and he often used ambush tactics and blitz attacks to outflank and surround his enemy. He seldom lost a battle. At the age of twenty-six (following the death of his father and brother-in-law), Hannibal took command of the Carthaginian army in Spain.

The young general had not forgotten his promise to his father. In 219 BC he deliberately provoked Rome by breaking the terms of the peace treaty and capturing the Roman trading port of Saguntum in Spain. When Roman troops arrived to arrest him, he was nowhere to be seen!

Hannibal had long dreamed of invading Italy. He knew that he could not safely move his men by sea, since the Roman fleet now ruled the Mediterranean, and so he decided upon an overland route. The Romans would never expect such an invasion, given the difficulty of moving a large mass of men and animals over the high mountains and wide rivers that lay between Spain and Italy. Should he be able to accomplish such a feat, Hannibal would certainly gain the advantage of surprise. He assumed that once he entered Italy, he would be supported by the Gauls living in the Po Valley as well as the numerous Italian tribes that had been conquered by the Romans. It seemed only logical to him that these people would hate their Roman overlords and hasten to join him.

A Carthaginian victory over Rome seemed a distinct possibility. And so, when the Roman soldiers arriving in Spain inquired as to the whereabouts of Hannibal, he had already begun his overland march to Italy.

The Long March

Hannibal set out in 218 BC with sixty thousand mercenaries (mostly Spaniards and Africans), nine thousand horses and thirty-seven war elephants. On the march, his army was seven miles long! After crossing the Pyrenees Mountains they moved into Gaul (modern France). The Rhone River posed a major obstacle, particularly for the transport of the elephants. Hannibal's men cut down trees growing near the riverbank and constructed large rafts. Then they led the elephants onto them. The movement of the rafts caused a few of the giant creatures to panic. They jumped overboard and walked the rest of the way along the bottom of the river with the tips of their trunks above the water! Other rafts were built for the soldiers, but the horses had to swim.

Only fifteen days were spent crossing the Alps, but this was the hardest part of the journey. The soldiers had to be on the constant lookout for mountain people, who threw stones on them from above. There were, of course, no roads, and men as well as animals frequently lost their footing on the narrow, winding paths and plunged thousands of feet to their deaths. Huge chunks of ice often blocked the way. When this happened, Hannibal ordered his men to pour vinegar over the ice, causing it to crack. The smaller pieces were then easily pushed aside. Sometimes the soldiers had to build huge fires to melt the larger icy barriers. The elephants were used to a temperate climate and suffered greatly from the cold. Finally, exhausted and half-starved, twenty-three thousand of the original sixty thousand men entered the Po River valley in northern Italy. They had completed the difficult march in only five months.

fig. 16 — **a war elephant**

The Second Punic War

Just as Hannibal had hoped, most of the Roman army was abroad, and the troops left behind in Italy were taken entirely by surprise. His plans to attract the Gauls to his side were fulfilled, although not every warrior joined his army. When the Roman consuls heard of his entry into Italy, they hurried north. They were so eager to destroy the invading army that they did not adequately scout the area, and when they attacked the Carthaginians on the bank of the Trebbia River, the morning mists rising from the water hid the ambush that Hannibal had cleverly laid. The Roman troops did not see the trap until it was too late, and Hannibal deftly outflanked and surrounded them. Only one third of the Roman soldiers survived the attack. Afterwards, Hannibal ordered his men to gather up the abandoned Roman weapons for their own use.

The Carthaginians were now masters of northern Italy, although most of the citizens of Rome did not know this. The Roman generals had escaped unharmed from the battlefield, and when they returned to the capital they announced that their side had won! It is unclear whether they did this to avoid lowering the morale of the people or simply to hide the embarrassment of their defeat.

Hannibal moved his army south toward a pass in the Apennines near the modern city of Florence. This route forced him to lead his men through the marshes of the Arno River, and he contracted a disease there which cost him the sight in one eye. For a while, he had to be carried on the back of his one surviving elephant (all the others had died after their long ordeal in the mountains). When he recovered, Hannibal planned his next trick. He enticed the Roman army (led by the consul Flaminius) to the north shore of Lake Trasimene. Once again, the morning mists were to play a crucial role. The Roman soldiers could see little as they marched through the damp air along the lake until the sun broke through and burned off the mist: Imagine their despair when they realized that there were Carthaginian troops ahead of them, behind them, and beside them! No Roman soldier survived this battle, but Hannibal did allow some of the Italian allies to flee. He hoped his gesture of generosity would win their cities to his side. Meanwhile, once the Roman senators had recovered from the shock of their defeat, they chose Quintus Fabius Maximus to serve as Dictator.

Hannibal then marched triumphantly southward, and crossed the mountains into the plain of Campania. This was now a prosperous farming region of vineyards and orchards. Fabius set up an army camp in the hills east of Campania. Since it had become clear to him that Hannibal was a formidable adversary with whom direct encounters should be avoided if at all possible, Fabius ordered his soldiers to attack only the small detachments of men that Hannibal sent out for food. He hoped to slowly wear out his foe by this constant harassment. The Romans called Fabius "the Delayer." Today the term "Fabian Tactics" refers to the strategy of exhausting an opponent through a constant barrage of minor attacks.

By the early fall, Hannibal began to make plans to lead his men into the hills to establish winter quarters. He could hardly remain in Campania, where every city was fortified and held by the Romans. Meanwhile, Fabius waited patiently, hoping to pick off Hannibal's marching soldiers once his cavalry had been sent ahead to scout the area. One dark night, a Roman sentry noticed a group of lights moving toward a mountain pass to the east of the plain. He alerted his officers, and before long the Roman army was marching in the direction of the lights. When the sun came up, the Romans discovered to their shock (and embarrassment!) that they had been following the lighted torches tied to the horns of a herd of cattle! Meanwhile, the wily Hannibal and his men had slipped out of Campania through a different pass! He had outsmarted them again!

The following spring (216 BC), the Romans elected two new consuls— Lucius Aemilius Paullus and Gaius Terentius Varro. Together they led an army of about sixty thousand troops to Cannae (near the eastern coast of Italy) where Hannibal was camped. They were determined to wipe out the invading army once and for all. By now it was summer. This time the Romans did not have to worry about morning mists as they moved across the hot open plain of Apulia. And they outnumbered the Carthaginian army at least two to one. Hannibal, however, had some cards up his sleeve. Observing that the wind was behind him, he quickly lined up his men with his excellent cavalry protecting the two flanks. Suddenly they charged, driving the dust into the faces of the Roman soldiers! And there was more to come. Hannibal had deliberately placed his weakest fighters in the center, so when the Romans lunged forward in a wedge-shaped formation, his front line was transformed into an inverted arc. Slowly, the unwary Roman soldiers were drawn into the center of Hannibal's army. Then the trap was sprung! Hannibal ordered his pikemen on the two flanks to swing inward and attack, while the cavalry chased off the Roman horsemen and then charged at the foot-soldiers marching in the rear. The surrounded army was then slaughtered in one of the worst defeats in Rome's history. Over fifty thousand Roman soldiers died.

At this point, the victorious Hannibal might have marched on to Rome, but he chose not to. According to legend, Maharbal, the commander of his cavalry, said to Hannibal, "You know how to win a fight. But you don't know how to use your victory!" Should he have attacked the city? Probably not. After all, there were other Roman troops ready to defend Rome, and besides, Hannibal had no siege weapons. Nor did he have a source of supplies and food.

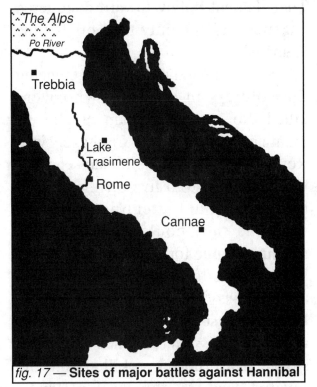

fig. 17 — **Sites of major battles against Hannibal**

After the disaster at Cannae, the Romans resumed the tactics of Fabius; flurries of surprise attacks followed by swift withdrawals deprived Hannibal of the opportunity to fight a major battle. For the next thirteen years, the Roman soldiers dogged Hannibal, ambushing his men and then disappearing into the countryside as he marched around Italy.

Hannibal's plan to break up the Italian confederation by winning the support of Rome's former enemies never worked out. Although Capua (the largest city in Campania) and many smaller cities in southern Italy backed the Carthaginians, most of the allies in central Italy remained loyal to Rome. Their lenient policy toward conquered enemies had certainly paid off for the Romans!

Hannibal had no means of replacing the soldiers in his army who were killed. Nor could he obtain supplies of grain and weapons from Carthage, since Rome controlled all the Italian seaports. His soldiers had to live off the land as best they could, stealing whatever weapons they could find. His one remaining hope for fresh troops was his brother Hasdrubal, who led a small army across the Alps into Italy in 207 BC. But as soon as the Romans heard about this mission, they sent troops to stop it. Hasdrubal was killed, and his severed head was thrown into Hannibal's camp in southern Italy.

Hannibal remained in Italy for fifteen years, valiantly leading his dwindling army against the toughest soldiers in the ancient world. His presence was a nagging thorn in the side of the proud Roman Republic. Although he was unable to attack Rome, he continued to wreak havoc throughout the countryside. Once he came within sight of the city walls and pitched his tents there. The Romans were understandably uneasy, but in a gesture of defiance they held an auction for Hannibal's campsite. It was allegedly sold for a very high price!

Meanwhile, the Roman general Publius Cornelius Scipio took an army to Spain and drove the Carthaginians out of the country. In 204 BC he landed his troops near the city of Carthage. In less than a year, Carthage sued for peace. The Romans agreed to negotiate a settlement IF they would call Hannibal home. The strategy worked: At last Rome was freed from the ravages of one of history's most persistent adversaries.

Soon after his return to Carthage, war broke out again. In 201 BC the armies of Scipio and Hannibal met at Zama, a town on the African plains; it was a five-day march (seventy-five miles) southwest from Carthage. Many of the soldiers who fought for Hannibal at Zama were veterans of his trek over the Alps sixteen years before. The Carthaginian army fought fiercely, but Hannibal no longer had the exceptional cavalry that had helped him win so many victories abroad (they had been conveniently detained in Italy). And so

Hannibal suffered his first defeat. It was also his last.

The second Punic War was over. Spain became a Roman province. The Carthaginians relinquished their war elephants, and they watched helplessly as all but ten of their fine ships were set on fire. They had to promise never to rebuild their army or navy, and they were specifically forbidden to wage war—even a defensive one—without Rome's permission. The once mighty Carthaginian Empire was reduced to the region of modern Tunisia, and Carthage itself became a tribute-paying ally of Rome.

Hannibal's Last Days

Hannibal was not about to retire from public life, however. As an influential leader in his government, he introduced many reforms that restored the economic prosperity of the city of Carthage. But he had many rivals who conspired against him, and in 195 BC the Romans ordered his arrest. It is a sad commentary that the man who had fought so brilliantly against his enemies was forced to flee from his own city. He lived for a number of years in Asia Minor with a Greek king, but he was constantly hunted by his old enemies. Finally, in 182 BC he took poison to avoid capture. He was sixty-five years old.

Fighting In Greece

After the second Punic War, Rome's attention was drawn toward the east, where King Philip V of Macedonia was boldly extending his frontier into Greece. In 197 a brilliant young consul named T. Quinctius Flaminius won an impressive victory against King Philip on the hillside of Cynoscephalae. In the treaty that followed his defeat, Philip agreed to stay out of Greece. When King Perseus (Philip's successor) disregarded the terms of the Roman treaty, Aemilius Paullus led his legions east. The two armies came to blows at Pydna, a plain dominated by the craggy heights of Mt. Olympus. When it was all over, twenty thousand of Perseus' men lay dead on the battlefield. The Romans lost only one hundred soldiers. Macedonia became a Roman province in 148 BC.

But there were still rumblings among the Greeks. When a rebellion broke out, the Romans advanced toward Corinth, the richest city in Greece, and totally destroyed it. Imagine the enormous booty they acquired there! Greece was soon added to the rapidly expanding Roman Empire as the province of Achaea (in 146 BC). The Greek states were forced to send hostages to Rome as a guarantee for their good political behavior. Among them was a scholar named Polybius (see page 25); he would later write a remarkable military history of Greece and Rome. Many other Greek artists and scholars emigrated to Rome at this time, and their influence upon Roman civilization was enormous, as we shall see.

Carthage Is Destroyed

Despite the loss of her empire, Carthage remained a prosperous trading city, and this made certain Romans uneasy. Senator Marcus Porcius Cato always concluded his speeches, regardless of the subject, with the words *Carthago Delenda est* (Carthage must be destroyed!). In this way, he kept alive the bad feelings toward Carthage. Inevitably, Rome picked a quarrel with Carthage, laid a siege, and finally destroyed the city. This is called the Third Punic War (149-146 BC), although it was really more of a massacre than a war. To symbolize the utter destruction of the city that had once challenged Rome, salt was poured upon its fields. Carthage and the region around it (modern Tunisia) became the new Roman province of Africa.

A Roman Lake

After the Third Punic War, Rome conquered the western coast of Asia Minor and made this area its sixth province (Asia). Thus, by 100 BC Rome controlled much of the land around the Mediterranean. The vast sea was becoming a Roman lake, as the Republic expanded into a sprawling empire.

Questions:

1. How did the Punic Wars get their name?
2. Why did Carthage have such a powerful navy?

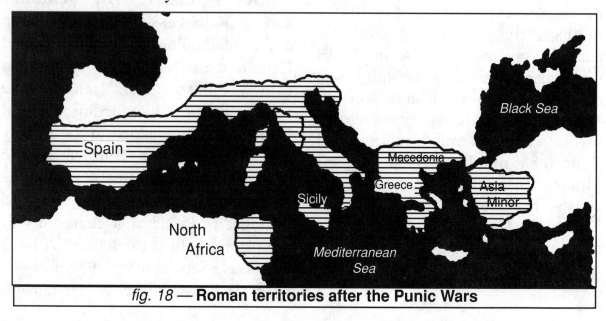

fig. 18 — **Roman territories after the Punic Wars**

3. What caused the outbreak of the First Punic War?

4. What was a corvus and how did it work?

5. Why did Hannibal lead his troops along the overland route to Italy?

6. Give two examples of Hannibal's trickery.

7. How did Hannibal win the Battle of Cannae?

8. How was Hannibal finally driven out of Italy?

9. What is the meaning of these Latin words: *Carthago delenda est*?

Ideas to Think About:

1. Although Carthage was a prosperous and thriving nation, there were many primitive aspects to its culture. For example, the noble families traditionally sacrificed their first born baby to the god Baal Hammon. The child was placed upon a sloping altar below a statue of the god; he then rolled down into a raging fire to be burned alive! Archaeologists have found small urns containing the ashes of hundreds of babies beneath identifying stone stelae (tombstones).

2. Despite its obvious advantages, the corvus was heavy and awkward, and it was never used again after the Punic Wars. As we know, the Romans really preferred to fight on the land, and since there were no longer any big enemy fleets to worry about, their navy slowly deteriorated. As a result, piracy increased dramatically!

3. The Roman provinces were governed by important magistrates. Once a territory was under Roman control, a governor (usually a former consul who was called a pro-consul) was sent from Rome with an army to establish law and order. His term was one year. But although the pro-consul was responsible to the Senate, Rome was very far away. As a result, he was something like an uncrowned king of the territory, and the temptation to enrich himself was great. Often a pro-consul imposed heavy taxes on the local people and pocketed at least part of the money himself. The Romans used to say that a new pro-consul had to have three times as much money as he needed to live: one third to bribe the local government officials, one third to pay off the great bills he would accumulate, and one third to bribe the court that would try him on his return to Rome! Needless to say, the governors were not well loved by the provincial people.

4. It is remarkable that Rome, with no naval tradition, came to dominate the seas. Equally remarkable is the fact that Carthage, with no military history and a reliance upon mercenary troops, should produce two of the most brilliant gener-

als of the ancient world, Hamilcar and Hannibal.

5. Despite the destruction of Carthage, the Romans could not ignore the strategic setting of the city. Eventually, Carthage became a great city again. But this time it was a Roman city!

6. The Greek historian Polybius witnessed the burning of Carthage, and he heard the Roman general (Scipio) express his fears that a similar fate might await Rome: "All cities...," he said, "must, like men, meet their doom."

Projects:

1. The siege of Carthage lasted three years. The people turned their temples into arsenals and made three hundred swords a day. Slaves fought beside their masters. In the end, a hundred thousand died. Find out more about the Third Punic War and write a short report.

2. Hannibal's hero was Alexander the Great. Find out who this great conqueror was and write a short report. Be sure to compare the military strategies of Hannibal and Alexander in your report.

3. Imagine that Hannibal was Roman, not Carthaginian. Write a short biography of his life as a Roman citizen as you think it might have been. Use your imagination, and back up your ideas with facts.

4. Regulus was a general captured by the Carthaginians, who sent him to Rome with their envoys. What was his mission, and how did he carry it out? (Remember the honor and patriotism of Roman citizens!) Write a short report.

5. Although Carthage was a powerful commercial empire, its culture was not distinguished by accomplishments in the arts. As we just learned, the Carthaginians practiced human sacrifice, and they were harsh in their treatment of the people they conquered. Given this information, are you glad that the Romans won the Punic Wars? Why, or why not? Write a short report expressing your opinion.

6. In 133 BC the prosperous kingdom of Pergamum in northwestern Asia Minor was bequeathed by its king to Rome. Find out about Pergamum. Write a short report about it, and be sure to explain why, in the end, it was simply handed over to the Romans.

7. Hannibal's brilliant tactics at Cannae have been copied by many military leaders. In 1942 General George Patton applied them in northern Africa. Find out more about this battle of World War II and write a short report.

Chapter V — The Religion of the Romans

The Numina

The early Latins believed that nature spirits called *numina* inhabited the fields, springs, rivers, trees, wind, and nearly every other aspect of the environment. These supernatural beings supposedly controlled the harvest, storms and floods, birth and death, the outcome of war, and the patterns of everyday life. The simple farmers did not understand how or why the numina caused events to occur, but they hoped that by pleasing them they could escape unpleasant happenings and perhaps even be rewarded with a rich harvest or a healthy child. The Latin word *religio* refers to this relationship between men and the spirits, and it is the basis of our modern word "religion."

During religious festivals, the farmers would often kill some of their prized animals and lay the carcasses upon an altar as offerings to particular spirits. Then a priest would step forward and utter prayers, imploring the numina to accept the sacrifices and be pleased by them. And so, from the start, the Roman religion was based upon rituals in which the people bargained with supernatural beings in order to avoid misfortune and to obtain specific favors.

Family Gods

The household was the center of Roman life, and from earliest times the people believed it was protected by special spirits. The *lares*, for example, guarded the family luck. Every house had a shrine called a *lararium* which resembled a small cupboard and stood in a corner of the main room. It contained small statues representing the lares; once a day the family placed offerings of food, wine, and incense on a shelf of the lararium for the spirits.

Some lares were believed to live in the fields surrounding the family home. To honor these spirits, a farmer traditionally built a small shrine with an altar at the boundary of his land. In January, during the festival of Compitalia, he placed a plough beside the altar, along with a group of woolen dolls (each representing one member of his family). This offering was supposed to guarantee a good growing season.

The *penates* were spirits that protected the storehouse, and they were worshiped to insure a plentiful supply of food. There was also a special guardian deity that bound one generation to the next. It was called the *genius*. The head of the family had his own genius, and when he died, his genius would be linked with that of his eldest son. The *manes* were spirits of the family's ancestors. Death masks (and later busts) of departed relatives were placed on a shelf by the family shrine, so that the manes could be included in the daily prayers. In many ways, these masks were an ancient version of our modern family photos.

The head of the family was called the *paterfamilias*. (We've seen this term before. In its plural form—*patres familiares*—it referred to the heads of the leading families of the early Republic.) The paterfamilias had great authority: He literally owned his wife and children, and his orders were never questioned. Each day he led the family worship ceremony and made the offerings to the lares, penates, and manes. For such religious events, he covered his head with the end of his toga (just as the priests did). He prayed to Vesta (goddess of the hearth) before each meal, and once everyone began eating, he threw some food into the flames in the hearth as an offering to her. Sometimes he used a special vessel called a libation bowl to pour liquids onto the fire; the smoke would ascend to the heavens and (hopefully) please all the spirits.

Other Gods and Goddesses

Some of the nature spirits were worshiped in many villages. Eventually, they would become important deities of all the Roman people. Jupiter, for example, was the powerful sky god. When the primitive farmers were frightened by bright flashes of lightening and loud claps of thunder, they concluded that Jupiter had been offended in some way. So they quickly offered him a prayer, and then made some sort of sacrifice to him as soon as they were able. Among the less awesome deities that were worshiped in many Latin communities were Pales, the gentle goddess of shepherds (the Palatine Hill was named for her); Flora, a goddess of flowers, fruits and the springtime; Tiber, the god of the river; and Terminus, the god of boundaries.

Janus was a two-headed god of gates, portals and arches. His two heads (actually two faces looking in opposite directions) symbolized a gate that is both an entrance and an exit. Later, a temple was built for him in Rome; its doors were kept shut in times of peace. Can you guess why? The month of January was named for Janus.

Other spirits were responsible for the more intangible aspects of life: Fortuna was the goddess of luck, Pietas was the god of duty, and Concordia was the goddess of peaceful cooperation. It is easy to recognize the modern English words that are derived from the names of these Latin nature gods.

fig. 19 — **Janus, the two-headed god**

The Greek Pantheon

As we have learned, the Etruscans brought the Greek religion to Rome. The Greeks believed that a family of powerful gods and goddesses lived on Mt. Olympus, a tall, cloud-covered mountain in northeastern Greece. These deities had human-like form, and a magical fluid called ichor flowed through their veins, granting them eternal life. Like the Romans, the Greeks thought that their lives were in the hands of the gods, and so they, too, made offerings in hopes of winning the gods' favor and avoiding their wrath.

The Romans saw many similarities between the Greek pantheon (family of gods) and their own deities. They lacked the creative flair of the Greeks, but, as we know, they were terribly adept at applying foreign concepts and doctrines to their own culture. It was easy for them to select what they considered the most important attributes of the Greek and Latin gods and then merge them, thereby creating a new family of Roman deities. For example, the sky god Jupiter "inherited" the characteristics of Zeus, the leader of the Olympians. Henceforth known as Jupiter Optimus Maximus (Jupiter the Best and the Greatest), he was king of all the gods; his special symbol (every god had one) was the eagle, which later became the standard of the Roman army. In a similar manner, Neptune, the Latin god of lakes and rivers, took on the attributes of Poseidon, the Greek god of the sea.

The Latin god of agriculture was Mars. Since the Roman farmers often fought to defend their fields, Mars was also associated with war, and this is how he came to be identified with the Greek war god, Ares. The Romans loved Mars and prayed to him before every battle. After a military victory, the army always marched to the Campus Martius (Field of Mars) to dedicate the booty they had won to him. Since the Romans fought only in the warmer seasons (in those days it was unthinkable to stage a battle in the wind and rain of winter), they named the month when an army resumed fighting after Mars (March). In later years, Mars became as important as Jupiter himself. (Did you remember that Mars was the father of Romulus

fig. 20 — Jupiter
H. L. Pierce Fund — Courtesy, Museum of Fine Arts, Boston

and Remus?)

Apollo, the Greek god of the sun, health, music and prophecy, entered the Roman religion without a change of name. The Greek god Hephaestus, the god of metalworking, was transformed into the Roman god Vulcan. Vulcan made thunderbolts for Jupiter under the frequently erupting Mt. Etna in Sicily. The word "volcano" is derived from the fiery site of his workshop.

Hermes, the messenger of the Greek gods, became the Roman god Mercury who controlled communications, trade and business. The logo of this god wearing his winged sandals and helmet can be seen in the modern advertising of FTD floral deliveries! Businessmen and traders paid ten per cent of their profits to a shrine dedicated to Mercury. The money was used to pay for a public feast held in his honor every August 12.

The Greek goddess Athena's persona merged with the Etruscan deity Minerva, the goddess of crafts. She retained her Etruscan name. Zeus's wife Hera was associated with Juno (also derived from the Etruscans), the Roman goddess of marriage and childbirth and the patroness of women. She was the wife of Jupiter. The Greek Artemis became the Roman Diana, goddess of the woods, and Demeter became Ceres, goddess of the harvest. (Think of wheat cereals and you'll remember her name!) Aphrodite, the Greek goddess of love and beauty, became known as Venus (the mother of Aeneas). Vesta, the goddess of the hearth, was associated with the Greek goddess Hestia.

Over the years, nearly all the Greek gods and goddesses were transformed into Roman deities. This explains why the Roman religion seems so similar to that of the Greeks! On the opposite page is a chart showing the relationships between the Greek and Roman gods and goddesses.

fig. 21 — **chart of the Roman equivalents of Greek deities**			
Greek Name	*Roman Name*	*Domain*	*Symbols*
Zeus	Jupiter	god of heavens, ruler of the gods	thunderbolt, eagle, oak
Poseidon	Neptune	god of the sea	trident, horse, dolphin
Apollo	Apollo	god of art, music, prophecy	lyre, the sun
Hades	Pluto	god of the underworld and of precious metals	Cerberus (three-headed dog)
Hera	Juno	patroness of women	peacock, cow, pomegranate
Demeter	Ceres	goddess of the harvest	sheath of wheat
Hestia	Vesta	goddess of the hearth	eternal flame
Athena	Minerva	goddess of wisdom, combat, and crafts	aegis, owl, olive branch
Ares	Mars	god of war	armor, vulture
Artemis	Diana	goddess of the moon and the hunt	bow and arrow, stag, crescent
Aphrodite	Venus	goddess of love and beauty	swan, dove, myrtle
Hephaestus	Vulcan	god of metalwork	anvil

By the time of the Republic, the Romans had invented many heroic legends to link the newly defined gods with their own ancestors. The story of Mars fathering the twins Romulus and Remus is an excellent example of this. The Roman legends lack the poetic and artistic quality of the Greek myths, but they make up for it with the heightened sense of drama and patriotism they evoke in their glorification of the past. We have already learned how such heroes as Aeneas, Horatius and Cincinnatus embodied traits that the Romans most admired, including military valor (virtuus), disciplined obedience to established authority, and the religious faith that the gods will protect the city.

Vesta and the Hearth

The Roman family gathered each evening around the hearth. It was the source of warmth and light as well as the place where food was prepared. The goddess Vesta watched over the flames of the hearth and was considered one of the most important deities. As we know, the paterfamilias made an offering to her at every meal. The eldest daughter of the family had the duty of tending the fire of Vesta in the home. The undying flame represented the family's permanence. If the flame went out, the family would experience a tragedy (or so it was believed).

A public hearth was located at the center of every city, and beginning in the early Republic six maidens were chosen from noble families to guard the sacred flames of the hearth in Rome. They were called the Vestal Virgins, and they were highly respected. A girl was selected to be a Vestal Virgin at the tender age of seven, and she looked after the hearth for thirty years. She had to be very attentive, because letting the fire go out meant bad luck for the city. The Virgins were not allowed to marry; if they did so, they were buried alive! They lived together in a beautiful colonnaded house just below the Palatine Hill. After thirty years, a Virgin was given a large dowry and permitted to marry (most didn't). In time, the cult of the Vestal Virgins came to symbolize the invincible power of Rome.

The Temples

The first important temple in Rome was the one built on the Capitoline Hill by the Etruscans in honor of Jupiter, Juno and Minerva. It should come as no surprise that they copied the design from the Greeks. This impressive structure became the model for all later Roman temples.

Basically, a Roman temple was a tall rectangular building on a high base with steps leading up to the entrance. (In this respect it differed from a Greek temple, which was built lower to the ground.) Pillars supported a gently pitched roof. Within the building stood a statue representing the god, but only priests were allowed to enter this sacred inner sanctum. All public ceremonies were held at an outside altar in front of the temple, and the people often left offerings there—coins, jewelry, statues, wine and food. (see fig. 47, p. 117)

The Priesthood

Over the years, there evolved a hierarchy of religious officials. The priests were elected by the people in the same manner as civil servants and politicians; in fact, the Roman people saw little difference between the offices of politicians and priests. We have already learned about the pontifex maximus (the chief priest). Priests of lower rank called flamens tended the temples of particular gods.

Sacrifices were always an important ritual in the Roman religion. The best specimens of goats, cattle or sheep were fattened up just for the occasion. On the day they were sacrificed, the animals were clipped and brushed, and they were led to the altar adorned with garlands and ribbons. One priest slit an animal's throat with a special ceremonial knife, and then another priest called the haruspice opened the abdomen of the carcass to inspect the entrails. The shape of an animal's liver and the presence or absence of blemishes on it were believed to indicate the attitude of the gods about particular public projects or state policies. It was a bad sign if it was deformed in any way! (Animal livers actually vary greatly in color and shape.) Afterwards, part of the meat was burned as an offering to the god, and the worshipers ate the rest. (Animal sacrifices were about the only occasions when people of the lower class dined on meat.)

A pig or a sheep was always sacrificed before a wedding, and the organs were examined to determine whether or not the gods favored the marriage. If they did not, the family had to call the whole thing off!

As we have seen, the augurs studied the behavior of birds to determine the wishes of the gods (it was a good omen if the sacred chickens ate greedily!). During the first Punic War, the commander of the Roman fleet (Claudius Pulcher) had some chickens on board so that he could observe their behavior immediately before the battle. When the birds refused to eat (they were probably seasick!), the exasperated commander threw the birds overboard. When the Carthaginian fleet triumphed in the fighting that ensued, the Romans blamed Pulcher for their loss because he had insulted the gods!

The augurs also looked for signs from the gods in the flights of birds (in relation to the four quadrants of the sky), in the positions of the stars, and in the the patterns of thunder and lightning. They also interpreted dreams.

The haruspices and the augurs wielded tremendous power. Just imagine! They could prevent a battle from taking place simply by announcing that the gods were angry! Their influence on the political development of Rome cannot be overestimated.

Religion and Medicine

Roman medicine was closely tied to religion and superstition. People who were ill usually depended upon prayers and sacrifices for their recovery. On some rare occasions, herbs were used successfully to treat minor complaints, but most "prescriptions" had little positive effect. For example, the recommended treatment for a broken bone was to apply the ashes of the jawbone of a pig to the skin of the patient, and the remedy for a fractured rib was a brew of goat's dung mixed with old wine! Any patients who improved did so because their limbs mended naturally in spite of such "medicines." One of the few treatments that worked was spiders' webs soaked in oil and vinegar: When placed upon a small wound, this rather slimy material stopped the flow of blood in minutes!

Significant advances were made in medicine when the Romans conquered Greece. Asclepiades was a Greek who lived in Rome in 100 BC. He experimented with animals and concluded that the body was made up of tiny particles which, when they were not properly arranged, made an animal (or person) sick. He also distinguished between physical and mental diseases. Rufus, another Greek living in Rome, wrote that the heart pumped blood through the arteries. Many Roman physicians studied the works of Hippocrates, a Greek doctor who had lived in the fifth century BC. From his writings they learned to carefully study the physical symptoms of their patients and to keep records that could be helpful in future cases. In AD 30 Aulus Cornelius Celsus would write a long work called DE MEDICINA, chronicling the effective medical practices known at his time.

The best Roman doctors served in army hospitals, where they had plenty of opportunities to observe and tend wounds. By the first century AD they had successfully performed surgery, set broken bones, and amputated limbs.

Yet, given the generally poor quality of medical treatment as well as an ignorance of nutrition, the average Roman life expectancy was rather short: Less than half of the people lived to be fifty, one out of every three children did not survive infancy, and mothers often died from the complications of childbirth. Among the more common diseases of the times were tuberculosis, smallpox, rabies, tetanus, and malaria. Plagues often broke out and killed hundreds of people, sometimes thousands.

The Roman Way of Death

When a Roman died, the family immediately made a sacrifice to the lares to purify the house. As an extra precaution, the paterfamilias performed a strange ceremony in which he spat out, one by one, nine black beans, each time incanting some magic words! The purpose of this rather awkward task was to persuade any lingering bad spirits to be gone. Needless to say, the body was removed as soon as possible.

All relatives as well as the household slaves marched in the procession to a funeral pyre, and there were often paid mourners as well. In earliest times, actors were hired to march in the procession wearing the death masks of deceased family members; in later years, as we have seen, the masks were replaced by portrait busts. These statues were carried by the mourners. Since Romans placed great emphasis upon the family, it is logical that they tried to include many generations—living and dead—in such events as weddings and funerals.

After a funeral oration praising the accomplishments of the deceased, the body was burned. Fire was considered a powerful force against the dark influences that had caused the person's death. The ashes of the dead were placed in a clay urn and buried by the side of the road just outside the town. The Romans hoped that by burying the ashes they could prevent the spirit of the deceased from haunting the living—they wanted to enjoy fond memories about their departed relatives, not be frightened by their ghosts! Tombs resembling small houses were built for wealthy people, but most graves were simply marked with slabs of stone. The bodies of the very poor were immediately buried in the ground, since this was cheaper than cremation. Nine days after a funeral, a special animal sacrifice was made to the departed spirit of the dead person.

Every February (the month of purification) there was a festival known as Paternalia. At that time, families visited the graves of their relatives and decorated them with garlands of flowers. They left milk and wine to sustain the spirits of the dead.

The Afterlife

Like the Greeks, the Romans believed that after death a person's soul was ferried across a river called the Styx to the Underworld. But first he had to pay Charon, the ferryman; for this reason, a coin was always placed in the mouth of a dead body. Once across the river, he encountered Cerberus, a three-headed dog who prevented the living from entering the Underworld (and the dead from leaving it!). The record of the person's life determined whether his soul would reside in Tartarus (a terrible place) or Elysium (a heavenly land of eternal light and happiness).

Questions:

1. What does the word *religio* mean?
2. What was a lararium?
3. Who was Concordia?
4. Why did the Romans name a month in the early spring after Mars?
5. Who was the paterfamilias and what were his religious duties?
6. How did the Roman legends differ from Greek myths?
7. Who were the Vestal Virgins?
8. Why did the Romans burn the bodies of their dead?
9. Who was Charon?

Ideas to Think About:

1. Saturn (the father of Jupiter) was the god of the fields; he protected the seeds and also granted good health to man. Saturday and the planet Saturn are named after him. Saturnalia was a festival held in his honor for a week in late December, around the time that Christmas is celebrated. In fact, many traditions associated with Christmas actually date back to Saturnalia. For example, during the Roman festival the people decorated their houses, inside and out, with garlands of flowers. After a visit to the temple of Saturn (where a bull was sacrificed), a Roman family returned home for a great feast and an exchange of gifts. Slaves were temporarily given their freedom during the feast, and sometimes they even exchanged roles with their masters. The traditional main course of the feast was roast baby pig.

2. Aesculapius was a god of health and medicine (the Greeks called him Aeslepius). According to Roman legend, in 291 BC a snake (the god in disguise) was brought to Italy from Epidaurus in Greece. It escaped into the Tiber and went ashore on an island near Rome. The temple of Aesculapius was founded on the site, and this was later replaced by the first Roman hospital. The modern medical symbol of a serpent coiled around a staff is derived from the legend of Aesculapius.

3. Although the priests had a lot of power, there were certain drawbacks to their position. For example, a flamen of Jupiter was subject to a number of taboos: He was not permitted to ride a horse or to see the army in battle array, and he was forbidden to eat or even name certain foods, to pass under an arbor of vines, or to go into the open air without his cap! Apparently, these activities were offensive to Jupiter!

4. In the first century AD, a Greek army physician named Discorides wrote a work called MATERIA MEDICA that described six hundred plants and their medical properties. In later centuries, it became the chief source used in the science of pharmacy.

5. Many Greek physicians had a rather low opinion of the state of Roman medicine. In the second century AD, Galen (court physician to the Emperor Marcus Aurelius) would remark that the only difference between the Roman doctors and the soldiers was that the doctors killed people in towns and the soldiers killed people in the country-side! His writings became the standard text in medical schools in Europe until the seventeenth century.

Projects:

1. Here is a list of words that come from the names of Roman gods and goddesses. Look up the ones you don't know, and then use each word in a sentence. Indicate the Latin source of each word. Mercurial, saturnine, concord, augur, martial, cereal, genial, and plutocrat. Can you think of any others?

2. There are many books available containing myths about the Roman gods. Read three and write a short report about each one.

3. Find out more about the Greek god Ares and the Roman god Mars. Then compare them. What do the rather opposing portrayals of the two gods in Greek and Roman mythology tell you about the differences between those two cultures?

4. The Romans had many important religious festivals. Find out more about them. Make a chart indicating the names, purposes, and special ceremonies performed at eight or ten of these festivals. Also tell at what times of the year they were celebrated.

PART TWO — THE SYSTEM BREAKS DOWN

CHAPTER VI — A NEW SOCIAL ORDER

The Patricians Monopolize The Farmland

The long years that were spent fighting Carthage greatly altered the structure of Roman society. Let's look back to see how things had changed. The citizens of the early Republic, patrician and plebeian alike, were farmers. Some owned more land than others, but all shared a feeling of pride in their work and an unquestioning loyalty to their local government. When war was declared against a neighboring tribe, each man dutifully put aside his plow and took up arms. Remember Cincinnatus? In those early times, most wars were decided within a few weeks, and so the fields were not neglected for long.

The Punic Wars, however, claimed large segments of the soldiers' lives: The first war alone lasted twenty-three long years. As a result, many of the farms fell into disuse: When they finally returned home from the wars, most plebeian farmers could not afford to repair the damages caused by the years of neglect. Prospects were even grimmer in southern Italy, where fifteen years of fierce fighting against Hannibal had destroyed over two million acres of land.

The patricians, on the other hand, took advantage of the opportunity to expand their own property by buying up many of the small farms. Over the years, the number of small farms shrank drastically while the size of the estates of the wealthy grew and grew. By the early first century BC, it was not unusual for a patrician to own as many as four hundred thousand acres! The rich channeled much of their energy into the development and management of their land since, apart from politics, it was the only occupation that was considered proper for men of their class.

The Effects of Slavery Upon the Economy

The social structure of the late Republic was further transformed by the importation of huge numbers of slaves—the prisoners captured during Rome's overseas conquests. The patrician landowners found that the slaves were ideal farm laborers: They could be acquired fairly cheaply, they could be beaten if they did not work hard enough, and, unlike the Roman farmers, they could not be called away from the fields on a moment's notice.

There was even a change in the type of products grown in the years following the Punic Wars. Since huge quantities of wheat were now being shipped to Rome from Sicily, Sardinia, Spain and northern Africa, much of the Italian countryside was converted into olive groves and grape vineyards, as well as pasture-land for large herds of cattle.

Clearly, the typical Roman soldier who returned home after years of fighting the Carthaginians faced a disappointing future. The simple farming life he had fought so hard to defend was no longer available to him, and the wealthy landowners had little interest in hiring him to work on their estates, given the abundant supply of slaves. His only option was to move to the city to look for a job. But when thousands of returning soldiers made the same decision, Rome (and the other large Italian cities) became over-crowded, and employment opportunities there dwindled. To make matters worse, many of the city jobs had also been taken over by slaves.

Thus, by the late Republic, Roman society was mainly divided into two parts; a small class of wealthy landowners and a large class of homeless and unemployed people. In between these two divisions there remained a diminutive number of merchants, craftsmen, and small farmers still eking out a living. Gone were the days when every citizen worked in the fields. Now, while the affluent patricians oversaw the

functioning of their large estates (called *latifundia*) and the landless plebeians wandered about desperately seeking work, it was the slaves who tilled the soil and performed most of the menial tasks. In fact, as the gap between the rich and the poor widened, the slaves gradually became the backbone of the Roman economy.

The Rich Get Richer

The new territories Rome had acquired around the Mediterranean were the source of great wealth for the central government. Conquered peoples were obliged to pay huge amounts of gold and other objects of value as tribute to Rome, and such enormous quantities of treasures poured in that in 167 BC the Senate abolished (temporarily) all taxes in Italy. The government had all the income it needed! Of course, this policy greatly benefited the wealthy landowners, since they paid the largest taxes. This is a good example of how the Senate (made up mostly of wealthy landowners) often proposed legislation that was in the interests of its own members.

The Greek Influence

As we have seen, the Romans had derived much from Greek culture since the days of the Etruscan kings. But now that Greece was part of the Empire, its influence became even more profound. Army officers and government officials stationed in Greece expressed great admiration for the architecture, sculpture, pottery, philosophy and literature of that extremely creative civilization, and they brought home shiploads of Greek marbles and bronze statues. Greek artists flocked to Rome where their works were in great demand. And many a Greek slave was sought out to teach the children of wealthy landowners.

The Client System

Fortunately, the poor in Rome did not starve, thanks to a social arrangement known as the client system. In earlier times, the head of a clan had looked after his poorer kinsmen and spoken for them in the law courts. Now the patricians set themselves up as protectors (patrons) of groups of unemployed plebeians as well as workers who came to Rome from other parts of Italy. The duties of a patron were not only to represent his "clients" in legal matters, but also to distribute among them food or a sum of money with which they could buy provisions. He doled out his "gifts" every morning, and then he would stroll to the Forum, surrounded by his fawning group of clients. The more numerous his following, the richer the patron appeared to be.

For this reason, many patricians were extremely generous with their daily dole, increasing their clientele strictly for the sake of gaining prestige among their peers! There was a catch, of course. The clients were expected to vote as their patrons directed in the meetings of the Assembly, and this helped the patricians to maintain their authority in political matters.

The Gracchi

The obvious inequities of the Roman class system attracted many public-spirited citizens to political life. Two brothers, Tiberius and Gaius Gracchus, were greatly moved by the desperate state of the plebeians. They came from a wealthy family: Their father had twice been consul, and their grandfather was Scipio (Africanus), the very general who had defeated Hannibal at Zama. The brothers became spokesmen for the discontented masses, and they were each elected tribune (Tiberius in 133 BC and Gaius ten years later).

As we have learned, a tribune could veto a proposal made by a government official. Furthermore, any proposal he himself brought before the Assembly could become law if it was approved by that body. Thus, the tribunes had great power, since they could bypass the Senate completely. The Gracchi (as the brothers were known) tried to use this power to weaken the stranglehold the Senate had on the Roman economy and government.

Tiberius sought to break up the huge estates accumulated by the wealthy patricians and to redistribute the land so that the ordinary people could have some, too. As expected, the Senate (most of whose members, of course, were among the richest landowners) was outraged by his proposals. Tiberius managed to get the law through the Assembly, but when he stood for reelection, a senator killed him by clubbing him with a footstool! Three hundred of his supporters were also clubbed to death, and their bodies were thrown into the Tiber.

When Gaius became Tribune in 123 BC, he demanded an allowance of cheap grain for the poor, new employment opportunities on public works projects, and the granting of citizenship to most Italians. He, too, aroused the wrath of the Senate, and he was forced to flee from Rome. Just as he was about to be captured at a bridge over the Tiber, he ordered his slave to slit his throat. His head was then cut off by the Roman soldiers and brought to the Senate, which had promised to pay its weight in gold. Three thousand of his supporters were later slain.

The death of the Gracchi reveals how greatly the government of the Republic had changed. In the early days, a tribune's safety had been guaranteed and his authority was recognized. But now the Senate seemed to have unlimited power to do as it wished. Its members were no longer the patriotic farmers of the past but rather selfish aristocrats who were determined to protect their own high standard of living at any cost. The murder of the Gracchi proved that a man could no longer challenge the Senate on his own. He needed a strong force to back him up, and, as we shall see, the most powerful force in Rome was the army.

The Optimates and the Populares

A long period of social unrest followed the death of the Gracchi. The Senate itself divided into two groups. The Optimates were conservative men who wished to keep the government at the *status quo* (as it was). They believed that only the rich and well educated were capable of governing Rome. The word "optimate" means "men of good birth." The Populares ("those of the people"), on the other hand, were more liberal. They supported some of the ideas proposed by the Gracchi, such as land reform and grain distribution to the poor, although they did not seek radical change.

The Equestrians

During the late Republic a new social class began to emerge that would influence the workings of the economy as well as the government. Known as the equestrians (the knights), they were successful Roman businessmen who were not members of the exclusive patrician class. The term "equestrian" dates back to earlier times when only the rich could afford horses to ride in the cavalry.

The Reforms of Marius

Gaius Marius, a member of the Populares, was consul from 107 until 100 BC, thereby ignoring the long-standing Republican rule that ten years should pass between consulships. He was a plebeian who had become a military hero while fighting in Africa, and he was greatly admired by his soldiers.

As consul, Marius devised a plan that would aid the poor and strengthen Rome's defenses at the same time. Until then, only property owners had been allowed to serve in the army, and so Rome was becoming terribly short of soldiers. Marius recruited the unemployed farmers into the army and promised to reward them after twenty years of service with a pension and a small piece of land. This was a great opportunity for the idle poor, but it also led to an ominous transformation in the attitude of the Roman soldiers. No longer were they farmers defending their land. Now they were professional fighters whose first allegiance was not to Rome but rather to their general, since they depended upon him to make sure that they acquired a good piece of land after their military service. In fact, upon recruitment a soldier swore an oath of loyalty to his military commander!

Marius sometimes used the support of his troops to accomplish his own political goals. When the Senate tried to alter a law that awarded land to retired soldiers, he marched his men into the Forum and demanded that they reconsider the matter! Needless to say, the Senate gave in to Marius' demands, and the incident made it clear that the army was a powerful tool in the hands of a capable general.

The Social Wars

From 90 until 88 BC there was a series of battles fought between the Roman army and the soldiers of some of the Italian allied cities. The fighting occurred because the allied soldiers were denied Roman citizenship, even though they had fought for Rome during the Punic Wars. These conflicts are called the Social Wars (*socii* means allies in Latin). After many soldiers were killed, the Senate finally agreed to grant all Italians Roman citizenship. In this way, Italy became a unified nation.

Sulla

Marius' most formidable opponent was Lucius Cornelius Sulla, a general who was an Optimate. In 88 BC he became consul, and the next year he led his legions to an eastern province to put down a revolt. (Mithridates of Pontus had expanded his kingdom near the Black Sea into Roman territory.) When a tribune proposed that the army command should be given to Marius, Sulla marched back to Rome and forced his adversary to flee. Marius later took advantage of Sulla's absence to march his own army back into Rome. After ordering the execution of Sulla's supporters, he had himself elected consul (for the seventh time). He died soon afterwards (some say he went insane), and his follower Cinna took over his position.

Meanwhile, Sulla established peace in the east and returned to Rome. (Cinna was killed just before he arrived.) Sulla appointed himself Dictator, not for the customary six months but for life! He called for a large-scale execution of those who had opposed him, particularly the followers of Marius. Thousands of citizens died at the hands of Sulla's soldiers. Among the victims were forty senators. Sulla rewarded 100,000 of his loyal soldiers with land taken from the families of the slain supporters of his hated foe, Marius.

As a conservative Optimate, Sulla tried to "turn back the clock" and revive what he considered the strengths of the Republican government. To curtail the power of the restless masses, he prohibited the tribunes from introducing legislation, and he enlarged the Senate by adding three hundred men to its ranks (mostly equestrians). He increased the number of praetors, and ordered that the juries in the courts be made up only of senators.

In 79 BC Sulla retired to his villa in Campania. He had temporarily halted the dissolution of the Republic, but he had done little for the thousands of poor who huddled in the streets of the cities.

Questions:

1. Why were the returning soldiers unable to resume their lives as farmers?
2. How did the influx of slaves affect Roman society?
3. Why was less wheat grown on Roman farms than had been in the past?
4. How did the client system work?
5. How did the Gracchi try to reform Roman society?
6. Who were the Optimates and the Populares?

7. How did Marius change the makeup of the army?

8. How did Sulla obtain power over the Roman government?

9. What group was now the most powerful in Rome?

Ideas to Think About:

1. There were two categories of slaves: those who worked in the mines and the fields, and those who worked in the homes of the wealthy. The first group led difficult lives (they were branded and chained, and they were often beaten to death when they didn't work hard enough). The home slaves, on the other hand, (particularly the Greeks), were well treated and were counted as members of the family.

2. When Sulla returned from fighting in the east, he had the names of "the enemies of Rome" posted on whitened wood tablets in the Forum. Each man listed was considered an outlaw, and his murderer was to receive a reward upon the presentation of the dead man's head! Then (as we have learned) the property of the "outlaw" would be seized by the state. Sulla desperately needed the valuable property to pay his troops. Many innocent people were listed simply because they were wealthy!

Projects:

1. It has been said that Marius' reforms of the army destroyed the spirit of the Roman Republic. Do you agree or not? Write a paragraph explaining why you feel the way you do about this issue.

2. Mithradates VI of Pontus was a colorful historical figure. Find out more about his life and write a short report.

3. As we have seen, political parties are nothing new in government. What are the two major political parties in the United States today? Compare them to the Optimates and the Populares. Do you see any similarities? What are they?

CHAPTER VII — BREAD AND CIRCUSES

New Public Programs

As the misery and unrest increased among the people crowded together in the cities, the Senate hit upon a plan to avoid further violence. It consisted of a government-sponsored program of free "bread and circuses" for the poor. The "bread" referred to the dole of grain that had been previously handed out by the patrons to their clients. The "circuses" were public spectacles presented at huge amphitheaters and race courses. They were called circuses because of the round shape of the buildings in which they took place (the Latin word for circle is *circus*). Ever since those early times, "bread and circuses" has referred to the government policy of providing the people with food and entertainment to keep them from complaining.

As with the client system, the patricians found a way to personally benefit from this new program. They vied with one another for opportunities to finance extravagant spectacles as a means of wooing voters to their political campaigns. The more entertaining the event, the greater the number of votes a candidate would receive in an election. This was an early form of lobbying.

The Amphitheaters

Amphitheaters were built in many major Roman cities. These imposing stone structures had tiers of seats surrounding a central arena; they soon became the setting of bloody battles involving both men and wild beasts. Exotic animals such as leopards, lions, bears, elephants and panthers were captured in Africa and shipped to the Roman cities for the spectacles. They were kept in dark cages, poked at, and starved for days; when the miserable creatures were finally released into the arena, they were stalked by "hunters" (usually slaves) wielding spears, while the audience eagerly watched and cheered when a kill was made. Sometimes two different species, such as a bear and an elephant, were chained together, and the crowd screamed with delight as the frantic animals tore each other apart! The concept was not new. A century earlier, Scipio had celebrated his victory over Hannibal at Zama by a gory spectacle featuring forty-three bears and sixty-three panthers.

The word "arena" comes from the Latin *harena* which means sand; hundreds of buckets of this highly absorbent material were spread upon the floor of the central area to soak up the blood of the mutilated dead bodies in order to prepare the site for the next round of entertainment.

The Gladiators

The most popular event in Rome was the gladiator fight, a hand-to-hand combat to the death between two trained opponents. The gladiators usually fought in the afternoon, after the bodies and blood of the morning kill had been cleared from the arena.

This event had its origins in the Etruscan culture. Centuries earlier, it had been a tradition when an Etruscan chief died that his slaves were killed and buried with him. Over the years, the heirs of the deceased leaders began to question the practicality of this custom, since it left them with few personal servants, and so they began the practice of sacrificing some rather than all of the slaves at a funeral. But how to decide who lived and who died? The solution was to divide the slaves into pairs; each man would fight his "partner" to the death at the gravesite. In the end, the slaves who lost were buried with their dead leader, while the others survived to serve the new chief.

The Romans adapted the old Etruscan custom to suit their needs for public entertainment. They set up special schools in Rome and Capua (in Campania) where slaves and criminals were trained as fighters. One of the weapons used by these men was the gladius, a short sword made in Spain, and from this word comes the term "gladiator."

There were several types of gladiator; each was recognized by the way he was armed. A Samnite carried an oblong shield and a sword, a Thracian had a round shield and either a sword or a dagger, a retiarii carried a net and a three-pronged spear (a trident), while a myrmillo was armed with an oblong shield, a sword and an odd-looking helmet with a fish crest. Speaking of helmets, the headgear worn by most gladiators seems to have been designed more for show than for protection, since it was very hard to see through the visor.

fig 22 — **A gladiator's helmet**

To make the spectacle more interesting, a match always involved two different types of gladiator. The fights were rather violent, and as the blood spilled, the audience cried out for more! If one fighter was wounded, he lifted his left hand asking for mercy. The government magistrate in charge of the spectacle decided the man's fate. He would point his thumb down as a signal for the man to be spared (this gesture signified "sword down"); a thumb pointed up meant the man's death, a good decision from the point of view of the crowd. If a gladiator was well-known and a good fighter, he would probably be spared so that he could entertain the people another day. On the other hand, a severely wounded man would probably be killed, because he was no longer useful!

The best fighters were often awarded wooden swords. This was a high honor, and it signified that its recipient would never have to fight again. Those few gladiators who won their freedom in this way usually became trainers of younger fighters.

The Chariot Races

The hippodrome (a Greek word meaning horse track) was a large oval course built for chariot races. Teams of four horses pulled light carts made of wood and leather at breakneck speed seven times around the track. The hairpin turns were the most dangerous part of the race, and men as well as horses were often killed or injured when the chariots tipped over or collided. As many as twenty-four races might be run on a single day.

The charioteers, usually slaves, stood upright. Each man wore a tunic, a leather helmet, and leather throngs around his thighs and legs. He tied the reins around his waist and carried a dagger to cut them in case he was thrown from the cart. Otherwise he would be dragged to his death! Some charioteers became very popular, just as modern sports heroes do. And like modern thoroughbreds, each horse had a special name; a favorite was Sagitta (Arrow).

The Roman Baths

Not all forms of entertainment in Rome were violent. The late Republic saw the blossoming of the public bath, something akin to our modern health club. Admission was not free, but the cost was low (about half a cent). Patricians, plebeians and even slaves went to the baths on a daily basis. There were separate facilities (or separate hours) for men and women.

The Romans got the idea of the baths from the Greeks, who bathed in pools after exercising. The earliest

Roman baths were not much more than washhouses, but over the years they became more lavish. We will learn more about them in a later chapter.

The Tenements

After the comforts of the public bath, the poor had to return to rather miserable living conditions. The city of Rome was divided into blocks, called *insulae* (the Latin word for island). Each block was lined with cheaply constructed tenement buildings several stories tall. They stood so close together that the occupant of one apartment could reach out his window and shake hands with a person in the next building! The first floor of a tenement contained shops and rather pleasant apartments with running water for those who could afford the high rent. The upper stories became increasingly shabby as one climbed the stairs, the top floor being the worst. There was no plumbing on the upper levels, and although the tenants could go to a public lavatory, they usually emptied their chamberpots and garbage receptacles out the windows! There was little furniture, usually only a table and a bench. Most people slept on woven straw mats. The windows had no glass, and so in winter the wooden shutters were closed; this eliminated the draft, but it also cut out the light and ventilation.

The flimsy walls of the apartments often collapsed, and fire was always a danger when the residents cooked on their small metal braziers. The Romans dreaded fires, because they rapidly spread throughout entire blocks and could kill hundreds of people. According to the laws of the time, an arsonist could be burned at the stake, and someone who accidentally caused a fire was sentenced to a public flogging!

The Homes of the Wealthy

Situated among the tenements were the large and comfortable houses of the rich. Such a dwelling was called a *domus*, and it might take up a half or even an entire block. The design of Roman homes had changed a great deal since earlier times. In the days of the kings, a typical dwelling had only one large room called an atrium which contained an open hearth and, above it, an opening in the roof. The word "atrium" comes from the Latin *ater,* which means black, so the walls must have been blackened by the soot and smoke from the fire.

The Roman houses of the late Republic were modeled after those of the Greeks. They were made of brick that was covered with plaster; the roofs were made from clay tiles. Each domus had an atrium, but this room no longer contained a hearth; it did have an

1. shop
2. atrium
3. impluvium
4. bedroom
5. storeroom
6. tablinium
7. triclinium
8. peristyle
9. lavatory
10. outer storeroom
11. kitchen
12. summer triclinium
13 study

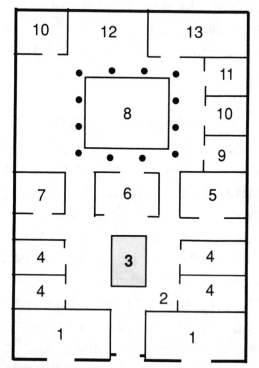

fig. 23 — **Blueprint of a domus**

opening in the roof (called the *compluvium*), which let in light and rain. The rainwater was collected in a shallow pool (the *impluvium*), which was connected to an underground storage tank from which the family drew its daily water supply. The lararium stood in a corner of the room. Surrounding the atrium were bedrooms, storerooms, a library, a kitchen, the *tablinum* (a room where guests were received), and the *triclinium* (dining room). A narrow entryway led from the street to the atrium. The front rooms were rented out to shopkeepers and craftsmen; they insulated the rest of the house from the noisy street.

The domus extended back to a courtyard and garden containing graceful Greek statues and perhaps an ornamental pool. A roofed colonnade offered welcome shade during the hot Italian summers. This open area was called the *peristyle*. A few rooms

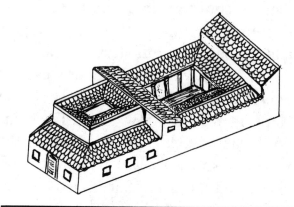

fig. 24 — **Outside view of a domus**

opened onto it, the most important being the summer dining room.

Even the wealthy Romans had few pieces of furniture by our modern standards: a few tables, several couches, some wooden chairs, beds and oil lamps for lighting. The lack of clutter must have made the homes seem elegant. Colored pieces of stone, clay or glass were arranged in patterns on the floors (these are called mosaics), and paintings (frescoes) decorated the inner walls.

As the Roman cities became more crowded, the rich increasingly sought the peace of the countryside. They built lavish mansions called villas on large tracts of land. Each country estate was like a small village, for it had its own vineyards, olive groves and fields of wheat.

The Polarity of Roman Society In the Late Republic

The contrast between the shabby tenements of the poor and the lovely villas of the rich dramatically reveals the degree to which Roman society had become polarized by the late Republic. And the gap between the small, comfortable upper class and the huge, disgruntled lower class continued to widen. To many observers it appeared that bread and circuses could not solve the problem of Rome's masses of poor and unemployed people. Another answer needed to be found.

Questions:

1. Why were the public spectacles called circuses?
2. Describe an amphitheater.
3. What does the word "arena" mean?
4. How did the gladiator fight originate?
5. Describe five types of gladiator.
6. What was a hippodrome?
7. Who went to the baths?
8. What were the insulae?
9. Describe the evolution of the atrium in Roman architecture.

Ideas To Think About:

1. Historians who later wrote about the gladiators got the meaning of "thumbs up" reversed. The source of the confusion appears to be an eighteenth century French artist named Leon Gerome whose famous painting POLLICE VERSO depicts the death sentence being given with the thumb down. The mistake was accepted by nearly everyone, and it has stuck! "Thumbs up" now means something advantageous for the individual involved.

2. In 73 BC., a Thracian gladiator named Spartacus led a revolt of his fellow slaves at a training school in Capua. He raised a huge army of

100,000 escaped slaves, which he hoped to lead to freedom outside of Italy. Spartacus held off three Roman legions before he was defeated (by a general named Marcus Licinius Crassus—we'll learn more about him later!). He and his men were crucified mercilessly (tied to crossed beams and left to die) along the roads leading to Rome.

3. The Romans later invented glass window-panes to hold in the heat in winter. Innovative experimenters used the glass in the world's first green-houses, where they grew warm-weather crops in the cold season.

Projects:

1. "The public spectacles provided a safety valve for public discontent." Explain in detail why this statement is true or why it isn't.

2. Using a shoebox and pieces of cardboard, make a model of a domus. The boxtop can be a removable roof.

3. Think of five English words that are derived from "domus." Consult a dictionary if you need to. Then use each word in a sentence.

4. The movie SPARTACUS is available at most video stores. Take it out and watch it. (Did you know that the word "video" means "I see" in Latin?)

5. Can you think of any examples in the modern world in which individuals or corporations fund extravagant "circuses" in the hopes of political or economic gain? Describe one example, and point out any similarities you see between the modern and ancient Roman policies of lobbying.

CHAPTER VIII — THE ROMAN ARMY

A Practical Approach

Rome grew from a cluster of villages to a vast empire largely because of the organization, discipline and strength of its army. As we know, the early Romans did not set out to conquer the world; they only wanted to protect and defend their borders. But on those occasions when they were drawn into battle they fought with incredible determination and courage. At the same time, the long tradition of the paterfamilias engrained in each man a respect for authority and a readiness to obey commands. Being an industrious and practical people, the Romans consistently applied the lessons learned on the battlefield to the basic training of their soldiers. Thus, the more the army engaged in battle, the more effective a fighting machine it became as new strategies replaced less effective ones.

The Army of the Early Republic

In the days of the early Republic, every Roman boy of sixteen attended a military camp for a year to master the use of weapons and to learn basic maneuvers. From then on until he was sixty, he could be called upon to fight on a moment's notice. Whenever Rome was threatened with invasion, all the farmers were summoned to the Campus Martius, where they gathered in groups called centuries. A century was about one hundred men (in Latin *centum* means hundred—see page 25 # 2).

Each soldier paid for his own equipment, and since the wealthier men had the better weapons, they fought in the front lines of the army. Those who owned horses made up the cavalry. The poorest men constituted the lightly armed auxiliary units. Sometimes they were armed only with farm tools! The officers were patricians. No man could become eligible for public office until he had served at least ten years in the army.

A New Formation Is Adopted

For many years, the standard military formation was the tightly-knit phalanx in which rows of soldiers marched shoulder to shoulder as a single unit. But the ponderous Roman phalanx posed no problem to the Gallic warriors who invaded Italy in the fourth century. Remember how they ducked beneath the solid line of shields and stabbed the Roman soldiers with their iron swords?

As usual, the practical Romans reacted to their unfortunate experience by finding ways to avoid similar disasters in the future. As Camillus pointed out, they needed a more flexible formation of soldiers, and so the army was reorganized into units called legions (each legion had about four thousand men). A legion was divided into smaller groups of one hundred twenty men called maniples. On the battlefield, each maniple arranged itself in three lines. In the front were the *hastati*, the strong young men. Behind them marched the *principes*, the more seasoned and experienced warriors. In the third line were the *triarii*, the old veterans who were called upon to fight only in times of great need. The commanding generals, of course, were the consuls.

Unlike the old phalanx formation, which could only move effectively on a wide flat field, the new, more flexible formation could advance and charge over rather hilly terrain. And it had other advantages. Whereas a soldier marching in a close-knit phalanx was allotted only three feet of space, he now had three feet on each side or a total of thirty-six square feet in which to maneuver and fight. As a result, fewer men covered more ground: 6,000 legionaries took up the same amount of space as a phalanx of 16,000! The improved maneuverability of the new formation more than compensated for the fewer numbers of soldiers in each unit.

New State of the Art Weaponry

Along with the new battle formation came an improvement in weapons. The cumbersome thrusting spear was replaced by the pilum, a seven-foot weighted javelin that could be thrown thirty yards. A hail of these javelins proved an effective means of breaking an enemy's charge. The pilum had an iron head and a shank of softer metal which fit into a wooden staff. It was designed so that the shank bent on impact and the head stuck in an enemy shield. Since it could not be easily pulled out, the enlodged pilum forced the enemy soldier to abandon his shield, thus placing him at a distinct disadvantage! Should a pilum land on the ground, it would bend in such a way as to render it useless and impossible to throw back at its owner.

The soldiers who fought in the Second Punic War had been greatly impressed by the swords carried by the Spanish soldiers in Hannibal's army.

fig. 25
A spear and a pilum

These weapons were forged out of steel in Toledo (a city in Spain). Such a sword (called a *gladius*) was virtually unbreakable, a quality that gave its owner a psychological as well as a physical advantage. It was relatively short, measuring only twenty inches. A gladius was sharpened on both sides, and this made it an excellent weapon for slashing and thrusting in close combat.

By the time of Marius, the steel sword was standard equipment for every Roman soldier, as were the pilum (each man carried two) and a short dagger (a *pugio*). For protection, the soldier carried a rectangular wooden shield (a *scutum*) covered with leather and bound with iron; a strip of wood attached to the inside of the shield formed a handle. On its slightly bulging face (the surface was rounded to deflect enemy blows) were painted the insignia and number of the legion to which the soldier belonged.

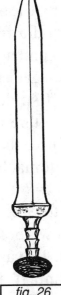

fig. 26
A gladius

A Professional Army

When Marius ended the draft (the required military service of all citizens) and began recruiting volunteers from among the unemployed plebeians, he created a huge professional army. The only qualifications for joining up were Roman citizenship, good physical condition, and a height of at least 5' 8". No longer did a soldier have to supply his own arms (the government took care of that), and he was paid a reasonable amount in Roman currency for his efforts. This removed the distinction between the rich and poor soldiers. And, of course, there was the promise of a piece of land upon retirement after twenty years of military service.

Every Roman soldier was issued a ration of salt. In those times, salt was used much more than it is today. It was especially useful for preserving meat and fish. The Latin word for salt is *sal*, from which derives our word "salary." This army ration is the origin of the old expression, "He is worth his salt."

The New Legions

Marius's reforms called for the organization of the Roman army into legions of five thousand men (all of them citizens). The ordinary soldiers were called legionaries and each legion was commanded by a general called the *legatus* (a senator). The legion was divided into ten cohorts of about five hundred men; each cohort was led by a military tribune (usually a young aristocrat). These, in turn, were broken down into six centuries of eighty men each plus officers. Two centuries were often combined to form a maniple.

The centuries were considered the major units of the army. They were led by centurions, ordinary men chosen by the legatus from the ranks. Their position was, in fact, the highest one to which an enlisted soldier could rise. The centurion demanded strict discipline, and this was symbolized by the vine staff he carried (and often used to beat his men). He oversaw the training of new recruits and personally set high standards in battle for his troops: He remained cool under enormous pressure while he encouraged his soldiers to hold the line. A centurion once showed his shield to his commanding general (Julius Caesar—more about him later) after a difficult battle; it had a hundred and twenty javelin holes in it! Despite the barrage of blows, the man had bravely stood his ground.

The smallest unit in the army was the contubernium, a squad of eight men who shared a tent in the camp, ate together, and fought side by side. They became very close and worked as a team on the field of battle.

The Roman army was indeed a tightly knit organization, and yet its flexible structure enabled the legionaries to form fighting units that were as large or as small as the occasion required. Let's review the divisions of a legion. Beginning with the smallest unit, a typical soldier belonged to a contubernium (along with his closest comrades), a century (the centurion was his immediate superior), perhaps a maniple (made up of his and another century), a cohort (led by a tribune), and finally the legion itself, under the command of the legatus.

The New Battle Strategy

A blast from a trumpet sounded the call to arms. Upon hearing it, the soldiers quickly lined up in the assigned formation. When they were ready to attack, they banged their pila against their shields; this must have made a deafening (and frightening) sound as it echoed across the field of battle! Another trumpet sounded the charge. The legionaries took a few steps and then hurled their pila, temporarily halting the enemy soldiers in their tracks. Then they moved in with drawn swords for close hand-to-hand combat. Sometimes, a soldier might rush against his opponent and knock him off stride with his shield; when the enemy threw up his hands to regain his balance, the legionary jabbed him in the stomach with his gladius!

The Roman soldiers came to excel at this type of warfare and few foes could withstand their assault. It was exhausting work, however, and if a soldier survived a battle for fifteen minutes, he was taken out of the line and replaced by the soldier behind him (who moved up to fill the gap). Thus, the Roman soldiers actually fought in relays, fresh fighters replacing the weary or wounded from what must have seemed like an infinite supply of men! No wonder the Romans managed to drive most opponents into the ground!

Every soldier was expected to fight courageously. Should an officer suspect a unit of cowardly behavior, he would drastically reduce their rations. If a mutiny was detected, every tenth man would be slain; the rest of the group then had to sleep outside the camp at night until they proved themselves worthy soldiers. This is the origin of our word "decimate"; it literally means "to reduce by a tenth," but its more figurative meaning is "to destroy utterly."

The Standards

Marius chose the eagle (*aquila*), the sacred bird of Jupiter, as the symbol of the legions. The standard of a gold or silver eagle mounted on a long wooden staff became a rallying point for the soldiers. Since those times, the eagle has often been associated with the power and strength of a nation, and it is the national bird of the United States.

Below the eagle were the letters S.P.Q.R. (standing for *Senatus Populusque Romanus*—"the Senate and the People of Rome"). The standard was carried by a special soldier called the *aquilifer*. He wore a bearskin over his shoulders, the paws crossing around his neck.

fig. 27 — Relief statue of a standard bearer
(Charles Amos Cummings Bequest Fund, Courtesy Museum of Fine Arts, Boston)

Every century, cohort and maniple also had its own standard, (usually a bull, ram or capricorn) placed on a long pole, along with other decorations symbolizing past campaigns and victories. The standard bearer of these units (called the *signifer*) was chosen for his courage and intelligence, because it was

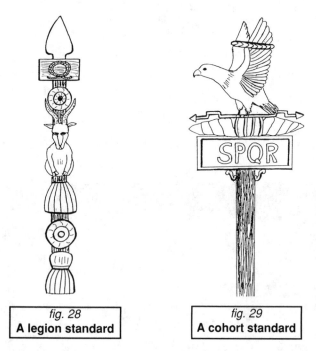

fig. 28	fig. 29
A legion standard	A cohort standard

up to him to keep the soldiers together and to lead them into battle. To lose the standard was a terrible disgrace. The cavalry carried a flag emblazoned with a colorful insignia.

The Auxiliary Troops

The legionaries were aided by auxiliary troops (non-citizens) who were recruited from the provinces. (The word *auxilium* means "help.") They were organized in cohorts of five hundred or a thousand men. It was their duty to protect the flanks of the legion from initial attack. Auxiliaries from certain provinces had special skills. For example, the Syrians were renowned archers, and the soldiers from the Balearic Islands (between Sardinia and Spain)

were accurate slingers (they fired off stone missiles from leather slingshots). The Roman cavalry was tremendously improved by horsemen from Mauretania (northern Africa). They patrolled and scouted ahead of the army, guarded the flanks in battle, and pursued retreating enemies.

Upon retirement from the army, the auxiliaries were given Roman citizenship as a reward for their years of duty. This was an attractive incentive, since Roman citizenship offered tremendous prestige as well as many privileges. Sometimes an auxiliary soldier completed his tour of duty in a location that was hundreds of miles from his own province; in such a case, he took advantage of Rome's excellent network of roads and walked home! In later years, soldiers from the provinces would fill the ranks of a significant part of the army.

The Soldier's Uniform

The uniform of a legionary of the late Republic consisted of a sleeveless coat of iron mail (connected links of metal) worn over a woolen tunic. (In later times, he would wear a leather shirt covered with overlapping plates of armor connected by metal hinges or leather straps.) His head was protected by a bronze helmet reinforced by an iron skullcap that was lined with cloth to make it more comfortable; hinged metal cheek pieces protected his face without blocking his vision or hearing. Centurians and other officers wore crests of horsehair on their helmets, so that they could be easily recognized and followed. In cool weather, the soldiers wore woolen cloaks, which doubled as blankets at night.

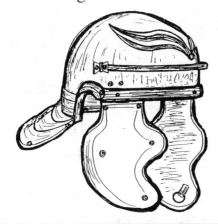

fig. 30 — **A legionary's helmet**

Legionaries wore leather boots (actually they were a combination of boot and sandal). They were called *caligae*, and their soles had iron studs

fig. 31 — **A legionary's caliga**

that were half an inch thick. The studs were supposed to keep the leather soles from wearing out too quickly, but even they wore down on long marches and had to be replaced regularly. An important army job was to restud the caligae. Some soldiers and officers wore molded pieces of armor called greaves to protect their lower legs, as well as arm guards.

Training the Recruits

A new recruit in the Republican army did not go to "boot camp" as modern soldiers do. Rather, he received his training at the camp of the legion he had joined, under the watchful eye of his centurion. He practiced running, jumping, and swimming (if a river was nearby), and he spent hours doing calisthenics. It was crucial for a soldier to be in prime physical condition. He also learned how to hurl a pilum.

The army employed some of the methods developed in gladiator schools for weapons training. For example, tall wooden stakes were set up in the parade grounds of the camp to represent enemy soldiers; each recruit practiced thrusting a wooden sword at them while carrying a heavy wicker shield. When the centurion was satisfied with a young man's progress, he gave him permission to participate in mock battles with his fellow recruits, using a real sword that was tipped with leather to avoid injury.

The Camp

The Romans placed great value upon a strongly fortified army camp. Whether he was on the march, fighting a war, or permanently stationed in a foreign territory, a legionary always slept in a well protected and organized camp that he had helped to build. An army on the march had to choose a new site each night. The ideal location was a hilltop facing the enemy with nearby supplies of water, timber, and grass for the animals.

The cavalry patrolled the surrounding area while the footsoldiers made the camp. There were a number of steps that they followed rigidly. First of all, they leveled the ground of a large square of land (one half mile on each side), marking the four corners with colored flags. Then they dug a ditch three feet deep and four feet wide around the perimeter. They pitched the dirt inside the square, where it was patted down to form an earthen wall (a rampart). Pointed stakes that were carried by each soldier were placed side by side on the top of the rampart to form a barricade. Lookout towers were spaced at regular intervals along the wall.

Once the protective barriers were built, a grid of wide paths was laid out within the camp. The main paths, which crossed at right angles in the center of the camp, were traditionally called the Via Principalis (running north and south) and the Via Praetoria (east and west). Leather tents were pitched in pre-planned locations around the headquarters of the legatus, which was in the center. Then each contubernium of eight legionaries laid out the straw mattresses in the tent they would share. Every centurion sited his own tent at the end of the rows of tents belonging to his century. If it was winter and the army planned to remain in one spot for some time, huts with thatched roofs were constructed in place of tents.

Building a camp usually took three or four hours, and once completed it provided the men with psychological support as well as physical shelter: They had a safe haven in which they could rest comfortably and a base from which they could launch the next day's operations. No one could enter a camp without a password, which changed daily and was passed from maniple to maniple on a waxed tablet. Of course, sentries guarded the camp at night; any sentry who was found asleep on the job was stoned to death!

In the morning, three trumpet blasts were sounded for an army on the march. The first was the signal to disassemble the tents, the second indicated it was time to load the mules, and the third meant it was time to get moving.

Permanent Camps

Should a legion remain in one place for a very long period of time (as we shall see, this happened more frequently in the later years of the Empire), the tents or huts were eventually replaced with timber-framed buildings. Many army camps that became permanent barracks were located at crossroads, near bridges or mountain passes, and near harbors. Local farmers and traders settled on the outskirts of such camps, and gradually small towns grew up; soldiers often retired to these towns when their duty was completed. In some cases, after the army moved on, the grid of the camp itself became the heart of a city.

On The March

The Roman soldiers trained hard. A legion that was camped for a long time in one location routinely made a march of about twenty miles at least three times a month; moving in close formation with six men abreast, they covered this distance in about five hours. When marching to a new location or to battle, they covered at least eighteen miles every day. This was a tremendous effort, because each soldier carried at least sixty pounds of equipment and supplies! This burden included armor, weapons, a sickle, a spade, an axe, a wicker basket, a cooking pot or two, three days ration of grain, a length of rawhide rope, and two or three wooden stakes for the palisade that was built around camp each night. It was Marius who ordered the soldiers to carry all this equipment, reasoning that the burden would make them strong and that they would always be prepared for any situation. This is why the legionaries bore the nickname of "Marius' mules!" Each contubernium was assigned one (real) mule, which carried tents, extra armor and siege weapons.

One reason why the army could march so rapidly was the network of straight paved roads that stretched across the empire. We will learn more about these roads in a later chapter. All that needs to be said about them now is that: (1) they were built by the legionaries themselves and (2) they enabled the army to get from one place to another faster than most people of the ancient

fig. 32 — A legionary

world would have thought possible.

A soldier's daily diet was simple: grain, which he ground up with a stone (or a handmill, if one was available) and cooked as bread or porridge, and any berries or nuts he could gather along the trail. He washed his meal down with cheap, vinegary wine. Soldiers on the march often pillaged enemy villages for extra food and supplies.

Other Duties

The army was up before dawn. Since the soldiers always skipped breakfast (they didn't know what we do about getting a good start in the morning!), they were ready to line up for inspection in no time at all. Then each man received a list of duties for the day. Among these were cleaning the barracks (and the latrine), repairing boots and studs, and polishing armor. The job the soldiers hated most was constructing roads and bridges: It was back-breaking work.

Attached to each cohort were builders, engineers, surveyors, medical orderlies, clerks and scouts. These men had risen from the ranks of the ordinary foot soldiers. They were not required to fight or to perform routine duties. (They were called *immunes*—what English word is derived from this Latin term?) In fact, Rome's best engineers, builders and surveyors were military men, and

they often accomplished amazing feats. A Roman legion once built a bridge across the Rhine River in only ten days!

The legionaries were never idle. When they weren't marching, digging ditches, constructing roads, or polishing armor, they were likely to be sowing seeds to augment the army's food supply. And, of course, they drilled constantly, marching in straight lines, turning from a column into a line of battle, and opening and closing ranks. A Roman historian once remarked that the soldiers' drills were like bloodless battles, and the battles were bloody drills!

The combination of rigorous training, strict discipline and unquestioning obedience to the commanding officers made the legions a nearly invincible force. Foreign armies must have trembled when they faced such a determined adversary!

Siege Machines

Sometimes the Romans besieged a city. This means that they surrounded it and cut off its food supplies. Waiting for the enemy to surrender to avoid starvation could be a long and tiresome process, however, and so in most cases the army resorted to storming the city walls. This required special equipment known as siege machines.

The Romans learned about siege

machines from (who else?) the Greeks, and (of course) they improved upon the original designs. The simplest device was the battering ram, a huge log cut to a point at one end (this was often reinforced with iron). Suspended by ropes from a wooden framework, the ram could be swung forward against the wooden gate of an enemy fortress. Each time it rammed the gate, the log swung back again like a pendulum and then the process was repeated.

The siege tower was a tall wooden tower built on wheels and covered with the skins of freshly killed animals (this made the tower relatively fireproof). Inside were steps or ladders. Once the tower was pushed against the wall of an enemy fortress, the soldiers hiding within dashed out across a drawbridge at the top onto the wall to engage in hand-to-hand combat with their opponents. The first men on the wall often won a prize

from their commanding officers.

The legionaries developed an ingenious formation for marching toward a heavily defended wall. It was called the *testudo*, the Latin word for tortoise. Marching in four rows of six men, the soldiers in the center and left of the testudo held their shields over their heads, those in the front held theirs forward while those on the right side held theirs facing outward. In this way, most of the unit was protected from enemy missiles by an outer shell of shields, just as a tortoise is protected by its shell. The left side and back of the formation were exposed, however, so perhaps the testudo proceeded forward at an angle.

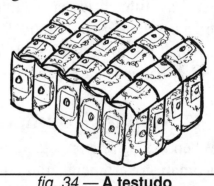

fig. 34 — **A testudo**

The Greeks had designed many weapons that worked by tension, using coils made from twisted skeins of sinew or human hair. From these models, the Romans created some interesting machines. The scorpion was a huge mechanical bow and arrow used to send flaming arrows into wooden fortifica-

fig. 33 — **A siege tower**

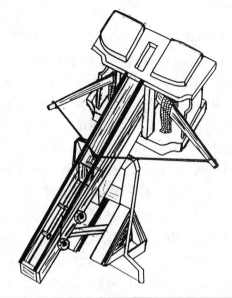

fig. 35 — **An onager**

tions. The ballista was a catapult mounted on a cart that resembled a giant slingshot. It hurled stones weighing up to sixty pounds over a city wall. The onager was a much larger catapult that hurled very heavy rocks and flaming logs. It had the force of a wild donkey, which is what its name means in Latin!

A Military Triumph

When a general won a great victory, the Roman government granted him a triumph: Riding in a chariot drawn by white horses, he led a parade of his soldiers followed by his chained prisoners and slaves carrying his booty down the streets of Rome to the Temple of Jupiter. Thousands of people would line the streets for such an event, shouting the praises of the conquering hero. Occasionally, the captured enemy leaders were actually strangled before the cheering crowds. A special stone arch was built for a triumph; it was carved with writing and relief statues commemorating the great victory. After the ceremonies, the prisoners of war were sold off as slaves.

A triumph was the high point in the life of a general. All too frequently, however, military leaders were so anxious to lead a victory march in Rome that they deliberately provoked unwary tribesmen. In later years, triumphs would be celebrated only by emperors.

Questions:

1. Why did the Romans discard the phalanx formation?
2. What was a pilum, and what were its advantages?
3. How did Marius change the makeup of the army?
4. Describe a gladius.
5. What were the main divisions of a legion?
6. What was the standard of the Roman army?
7. Describe the uniform of a legionary.
8. What did a legionary have to carry on a march?
9. List the basic steps involved in building a new camp.
10. What was a ballista?

Ideas To Think About:

1. During the early Republic, all Roman citizens were eligible to fight in the army, but not all of them fought at one time. The Romans devised a system to select soldiers for a particular time period. At the beginning of his term, a new consul chose his tribunes, who then selected soldiers for that year. All property-owning citizens were told to assemble on the Capitoline Hill. As they stood in groups according to height and age, the tribunes of each legion took turns choosing men, just as modern children in a playground select teams. This system insured that each legion had its fair share of tall, young fighters. Older, shorter men were chosen last, and when they did fight, it was in the back ranks.

2. The Spanish taught the Romans the art of making a steel sword (a gladius). To do this, a smith first took pieces of iron ore (rock with iron in it) and smelted it in a furnace to separate the metal from the rock. He then heated the metal and hammered it over a charcoal fire (iron doesn't get hot enough to melt completely, so it has to be hammered into shape), causing charcoal fumes to combine with the iron. The result was a steel blade.

Projects:

1. On a large piece of poster board, make a model of a Roman army camp. Use toothpicks or popsicle sticks for the tent poles and barricade. Clay or instant paper mache can be used for the ramparts, and scraps of cloth make good tents. Be sure that the grid is perfectly square. Consult the pictures in several books in your classroom or library before you begin.

2. The following Latin words were often used to describe the characteristics of the ideal Roman soldier: *fidelitas, disciplina, fortitudo, severitas, gravitas, pietas*. Can you determine their meaning?

3. What were the necessary qualities of a good centurion? What were the requirements for a good legionary? Write job descriptions for these two positions as they might appear in an ancient newspaper. Use your imagination!

4. The accounts of Polybius (see page 43) are a major source of our knowledge about the Republican army. Find a book that contains some of his descriptions and read them to the class.

5. On poster board, draw a chart of a legion, indicating the smaller units that made up the whole.

CHAPTER IX — CAESAR!

Growing Civil Unrest

By the end of the Republic, the difficult living conditions of the majority of the people living in the cities led to numerous protests, and violence frequently resulted. The old ideals of self discipline and loyalty to the state were nearly forgotten. Wealth rather than character had become the standard by which the men in power were measured, and the lower classes saw little chance of bettering their lives.

The burdens of those few farmers who had tried to make a go of it after the Punic Wars became intolerable as grain imported from Africa flooded the market and drastically reduced the price of local wheat. So while the large estates of the patricians continued to prosper with their vast production of grapes and olives (as well as animal products), the small wheat farms were simply forced out of business.

Furthermore, the unrelenting influx of slaves continued to absorb most of the jobs in the cities, although a small number of plebeians were able to thrive as weavers, grocers, fullers (cleaners), blacksmiths, shoemakers, and artists. It was common practice in those times for a patrician to buy a slave who appeared to be bright, set him up in a trading business of some sort, and then split the profits with him. In this way, the slave-owner could increase his wealth without becoming personally involved in business (an occupation considered improper for patricians). Many slaves in this situation were able to gradually accumulate enough money to buy back their freedom. The plebeian shopkeepers and artisans were at a distinct disadvantage, since they lacked the financial backing granted the slaves. How humiliating and frustrating it must have been for them to be bettered by Rome's captives of war!

The failure of the Gracchi to effect changes that would have given the poor a chance to make a decent life for themselves through a redistribution of the land and the grain supply left the lower classes with little hope, so fighting became an increasingly common occurrence among the people in the towns and cities.

Pompey and Crassus Become Consuls

When Sulla retired in 79 BC, there was a new struggle for power among the more powerful army generals that ended when Gnaeus Pompeius (known as Pompey) and Marcus Licinius Crassus forced the Senate to accept them as consuls (in 70 BC). Pompey was a brilliant general who had quelled a rebellion led by Marius' supporters in Spain. Crassus had crushed a slave revolt led by the gladiator Spartacus (see page 73). As one of the wealthiest men in Rome, he was constantly looking for new ways to fatten his wallet, and he loved to show off the riches he had accumulated (he once had a diamond necklace made for his pet eel!).

Pompey and Crassus restored the power of the tribunes and curtailed that of the Senate, thereby reestablishing somewhat of a balance between the patricians and the plebeians in the government. But they were unable to bring order to the cities.

In 67 BC Pompey was given the task of clearing the Mediterranean Sea of pirates. He accomplished this in an amazing ninety days! The following year he fought Mithridates of Pontus and conquered a sizeable territory in Asia including Armenia, Syria and Palestine. These victories won him great fame and popularity among the Roman citizens.

The Young Caesar

Gaius Julius Caesar was a nephew of Marius. He was born in 100 BC, the second son of a patrician family that claimed descent from Aeneas. Like most boys of his social class, Caesar was trained for a life of politics, and he studied Greek and Latin literature, philosophy, and rhetoric (the art of persuasive argument). He visited the Senate whenever he could, and he carefully observed the manner in which adept politicians won their arguments. In later years, his oratorical skills would serve him well.

In his twenties, Caesar was considered a ladies' man and a dandy, a fun-loving fellow who loved to give big parties. He was an attractive man: tall and muscular of build with a fair complexion and dark intelligent eyes. He was, in fact, rather vain in regard to his appearance. (In later life, his attempts to cover his receding hairline by combing his hair forward started a new fashion in mens' coiffure!) And he was a charming man—outgoing, witty, and extremely courteous. He had a keen mind and tremendous energy; when he decided to do something, he accomplished the task swiftly and efficiently.

Caesar married Cornelia, the daughter of the consul Cinna (Marius' successor). When Sulla declared himself Dictator for life, he ordered the public posting of the names of men who were "enemies of Rome" (see page 67, #1). Caesar found his name included on one of these lists and immediately arranged to see Sulla. The Dictator decided to be "generous" in this case, since the young man came from an influential family. He told Caesar that he would be spared if he divorced Cornelia (after all, she was the daughter of the associate of his great enemy, Marius). Caesar refused, and, recognizing the danger of remaining in Rome, he took his family to Bithynia in the province of Asia, where he served as an officer in the army.

The Beginning of a Political Career

Upon the death of Sulla, Caesar returned to Rome (after taking time to study rhetoric on the Greek island of Rhodes). He formally began his political career as a pontiff in Rome and then became quaestor in Spain in 69 BC. Continuing to climb up the political ladder, he was elected aedile (in Rome) in 65 BC. As aedile, he was responsible for providing the public entertainment (as well as maintaining the city buildings). This position offered him a golden opportunity to gain popularity among the Roman people, and he made the most of it. He sponsored wild animal shows and gladiator fights that were more spectacular than Rome had ever witnessed before. He spent huge sums of his own money, and then he borrowed more from Crassus, thus forging a bond with that greedy financier that would affect the political future of Rome. The next year Caesar was elected

pontifex maximus, and he probably exhibited his dramatic flair when he supervised the public sacrifices. He became praetor in 62 BC. and governor of the province of Spain in 61 BC.

As Caesar steadily advanced in his political career, he found himself in the advantageous position of enjoying the support of plebeians and patricians alike. Other high-ranking magistrates must have envied his ability to command the attention of the masses with his moving speeches (the people considered him a young Marius) while maintaining a comfortable relationship with the wealthy aristocrats who were his social equals. His political sympathies, however, lay with the Populares, and he was often exasperated by the conservative tendencies of the Optimates.

When his wife Cornelia died, Caesar married again. This marriage did not last long, however. He divorced his second wife (Pompeia) when her name was linked to a scandal, because, as he allegedly remarked, "Caesar's wife must be above suspicion."

The First Triumvirate

As consuls, Pompey and Crassus became concerned about the growing number of enemies they had in the Senate, particularly two Optimates named Cato (Marcus Porcius Cato) and Cicero (Marcus Tullius Cicero). Cato (called the Younger) was the great grandson of Cato the Elder (Marcus Porcius Cato) who had proclaimed so many times in the Senate that Carthage must be destroyed. Crassus also worried about Pompey's love of power, and he thought it wise to support the rapidly rising Caesar to counter-balance the clout of his fellow consul. Caesar could not have been more pleased! In 60 BC the three men formed the First Triumvirate, an extra-legal alliance in which they promised to help each other achieve their political goals. What were their specific goals? Pompey wanted to obtain a large portion of land for his retired soldiers, Crassus wanted tax concessions for himself and his fellow capitalists, and Caesar was anxious to see what it was like at the top of the vast Roman bureaucracy.

Pompey and Crassus used their power and influence to get Caesar elected consul, along with another man named Marcus Calpurnius Bibulus. During this consulship, Caesar showed little respect for the Roman constitution: He forced his ideas on the Senate and Assembly, and he intimidated Bibulus to the point that the poor man felt compelled to remain at home. (On one occasion when Bibulus argued against Caesar, a pail of excrement was dumped upon his head!) Caesar saw to it that his two allies got what they wanted, and he undoubtedly savored his first taste of power.

Governor of Gaul

It was a tradition that after his term of office as consul, a Roman leader became the governor (pro-consul) of a province (see page 45, # 3). This position was usually viewed as an opportunity to feather one's nest (become immensely rich) by demanding illegal taxes from the local population and then pocketing the money. After all, Rome was very far away, and it was easy to rule as one pleased in the distant territories. Every province had a group of tax-collectors called publicans, and these men often conspired with a governor to demand huge sums from the people and then divide the profits. This explains why the publicans are portrayed as such villains in the Bible!

Caesar, on the other hand, regarded a governorship as an opportunity to demonstrate his military ability and to gain the support of the Roman legions. He realized that he would need the army behind him if he was to gain absolute control of the government in Rome. With this plan in mind, he became governor of Gaul (a territory of warring tribes made up of modern France, Belgium, the Netherlands, and parts of Switzerland and Germany) in 58 BC. The land was rich in natural resources.

Before leaving Rome he married Calpurnia, the daughter of the man who succeeded him as consul.

The Gauls had been enemies of Rome ever since 390 BC when they invaded Italy and destroyed the capital city. The Romans had long dreamed of revenge, and Caesar was the man to achieve it. When he assumed the governorship, only the southeastern part of Gaul was under Roman rule. Caesar led his army into this territory with the announced intention of driving back the Helvetians, an invading tribe from the eastern mountains (the Alps). But once these intruders had been successfully dealt with, Caesar began a campaign to conquer the rest of Gaul. It took him eight years of hard fighting and brilliant strategic planning, but in the end he had subdued the entire province.

Caesar was a brilliant military strategist whose motto was *celeritas*! (swiftness). He had a knack for quickly sizing up a situation and then acting decisively. He called his men "comrades" and generously shared the spoils of war with them. He issued elegant gold and silver inlaid weapons to his bravest officers, and doubled the pay of everyone who had fought in the early battles. He tried to set an example of courage and tenacity for his men. If his legions reached an unfordable river, Caesar would dive into the water and swim, or climb into an inflated animal skin and paddle across. Of course, his men would eagerly pursue their leader. While fighting against a Belgian tribe called the Nervii, Caesar realized that his men were losing heart; so, drawing his sword, he plunged into the fray, fighting shoulder to shoulder with his troops. Such examples of personal bravery won him the undying loyalty of his legions.

Caesar found time throughout the campaign to write a fascinating account of his military experiences. Although this work (COMMENTARIES ON THE GALLIC WARS) was, in part, an effort to publicize his victories for political gain, it was so well written that it is still studied and appreciated for its literary merit today. It is also an invaluable source of information about the Roman army of the late Republic.

Vercingetorix

Caesar's most formidable opponent during his campaign was Vercingetorix, the fiery leader and hero of the Gauls. Vercingetorix tried to unite the various tribes living in the region of modern France, and he led many of them in an aggressive assault against the Romans. But after many battles, Caesar finally forced Vercingetorix to retreat with his eighty thousand warriors to Alesia, a fortified hilltop town. There he made his last stand.

Caesar carefully studied the steep drop-off of the cliffs and the huge stone walls surrounding Alesia. Deciding that the city walls were impregnable, he laid a siege. The Roman soldiers built a wall more than nine miles long completely around Alesia. It was twelve feet high and interspersed with eight camps and twenty-three towers that would hold catapults and archers. Then they dug two concentric ditches around the base of the wall facing Alesia (one was filled with water). The ground between the ditches and the city wall was strewn with booby traps (pits filled with tangled boughs and pointed sticks as well as logs implanted in the earth that were topped with iron hooks). A second wall was built outside the first Roman wall (it was thirteen miles long) so that

Caesar's soldiers could not be attacked from behind.

With this series of concentric barriers the Romans managed to completely isolate the Gauls. Vercingetorix could not hold out indefinitely without supplies and reinforcements, and his people began to suffer. But when groups of women and children poured out of the city begging for food, the Roman guards callously turned them back.

The arrival of a Gallic relief army must have caused Vercingetorix and his men to rejoice. These warriors began to surround the ring of Roman soldiers, preparing to attack them from behind. But the crafty Caesar had hidden his cavalry in the woods beyond the walls, and, at his signal, the Roman horsemen charged. Now the relief army had to fight the Romans on both sides. Vercingetorix sent his own men out the city gates, hoping that they would divert the Roman soldiers from their attack upon the relief army. But most of these warriors fell into hidden pits or were slain by arrows shot from the towers.

After much hard fighting, Vercingetorix was finally forced to give up. Wearing his finest armor and mounted on a prancing stallion, he surrendered himself to Caesar. He was later taken to Rome in chains; after parading in Caesar's triumph before

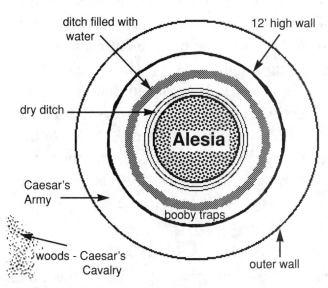

fig. 36 — **Siege fortifications at Alesia**

the cheering crowds, he was executed in his prison cell at the foot of the Capitoline Hill. To this day, that courageous Gallic warrior is considered a national hero in France. A statue of him stands on the hilltop at Alesia.

After the surrender of Vercingetorix, the Gallic resistance lost its punch. Caesar completed his sweep with a victory at Uxellodunum, where he ordered the hands of all enemy soldiers cut off "so that everyone might see how evil doers are punished." With the conquest of Gaul, the Roman Empire was extended northward to the North Sea and eastward to the Rhine River. Caesar's victories opened up much of western Europe to the influence of the ancient civilizations of the Mediterranean.

Apart from his military glory, Caesar also won great wealth for himself and his close associates by enslaving thousands of "barbarian" warriors and selling them at the Roman slave markets.

Crossing the Rubicon

When Crassus was killed in Asia in 53 BC, Pompey saw his power increase. But he was still concerned about Caesar's growing fame, and so he had himself designated sole consul. He then persuaded the Senate that Caesar was an extremely ambitious man who was capable of destroying what was left of the constitutional government of the Republic (as indeed he was). The senators immediately ordered Caesar to return to Rome—without his army. But Caesar distrusted Pompey, and he knew that his life would be in great danger should he return to the city alone. Yet, it was treason for a provincial governor to lead his soldiers out of his territory and into the city (the Senate remembered what Marius had done).

Caesar considered his options and decided to take the city by force. He moved quickly and secretly from his headquarters on the Adriatic Sea. Under the cover of darkness, he traveled south in a carriage drawn by mules that had been borrowed from a local baker. At dawn he arrived at the Rubicon, a small stream that divides Gaul from northern Italy. One of his legions awaited him there. It was now January 49 BC. As he led his men across the Rubicon, Caesar dramatically uttered (in Greek), "The die is cast!" He realized that his aggressive act could cause a civil war, but there was no turning back. When Caesar's army entered Rome there was little resistance; Pompey and his supporters had fled to Greece.

Dictator

Soon afterwards, Caesar hastened with his legions to Spain, where he defeated an army loyal to Pompey, and then returned to Rome. The Senate agreed to make him Dictator. He now held absolute military authority in Italy and all the provinces; he was master of an empire that nearly encircled the Mediterranean.

In 48 BC Caesar defeated Pompey at the battle of Pharsalus in Greece. Pompey fled to Egypt, but he was captured and beheaded on the orders of the teenaged Pharaoh Ptolemy XIII. Hoping to gain the favor of Rome, Ptolemy sent Pompey's head to Caesar. But Caesar wept at the sight of the severed head of his former ally.

Cleopatra

In those days, Egypt was an immensely rich nation; it was ruled by a dynasty of Greeks that had been founded by a general of Alexander the Great. The reigning monarch had just died, and his son and daughter jointly inherited the throne. The girl was named Cleopatra, and she was eighteen years old. Her brother, Ptolemy XIII of whom we have just spoken, had supporters who wished him to rule alone. Cleopatra was determined to hold on to her position, and she took advantage of Caesar's visit to Alexandria, the capital city of Egypt, to win his support. According to Plutarch, an Egyptian servant carried a carpet into the palace where Caesar was staying; he unrolled it, and out stepped Cleopatra! Caesar became infatuated with the charming girl, and he used his troops to help her gain the throne as Queen of Egypt and an ally of Rome. Ptolemy was conveniently drowned in the Nile!

Cleopatra (VII) was the last of the Ptolemy dynasty to rule Egypt, and yet the first in her family to learn and speak the Egyptian language. In fact, she spoke seven languages fluently, including Caesar's Latin. When she assumed power, she began to make plans to restore Egypt to its former greatness. Although she married one of her brothers, she fell in love with Caesar and they had a son named Caesarion (little Caesar). Caesar at this point was about fifty-two, and Cleopatra was twenty-one.

While in Alexandria, Caesar learned about the relatively accurate Egyptian calendar. He later instructed Roman scholars to reform the old Latin calendar using the Egyptian one as their model. The new calendar had 365 days, with an extra day added every four years. It was called the Julian calendar (after Julius Caesar). To start the new year properly (so that the seasons were aligned), the current one was made 445 days long. Although Pope Gregory further revised it in 1582, shortening some months, the Julian calendar is basically the one we use today.

Caesar also made plans to build public libraries in Rome based upon the one he had visited in Alexandria. (Unfortunately the Egyptian library was accidentally burned during the fight to establish Cleopatra on the throne.)

Return to Rome

After eight months, Caesar left Egypt and sailed to Syria. From there he marched across Asia Minor to Zela to drive back the army of Pharnaces, King of Pontus. (Pharnaces was the son of Mithridates, whose armies had been defeated by Sulla and (later) Pompey.) Caesar was puzzled and amazed when Pharnaces charged uphill against the mighty Roman legions; it seemed like a suicidal act! What could Pharnaces have been thinking? The legions duly attacked and easily routed the enemy. Caesar summed up the encounter in the famous words, "Veni, vidi, vici" (I came, I saw, I conquered).

After a campaign in Africa, Caesar returned to Rome. To his delight, he was welcomed as a great hero by crowds of cheering citizens. Four magnificent triumphs were followed by a forty-day festival of banquets and public spectacles held in his honor. He was reappointed Dictator, this time for a period of ten years.

Cleopatra followed Caesar to Rome.

According to Egyptian law (but not Roman law), he was her husband. Caesar installed her in a luxurious house beside the Aventine Hill. The Roman citizens greatly disapproved of this relationship (after all, he was married to Calpurnia), and they worried that his interest in Egypt would prevent Caesar from making policy decisions that best served Rome. They called Cleopatra "the Egyptian witch," but despite the unfriendly treatment, she remained in Rome.

In 44 BC Caesar was made Dictator for life. He began to wear a purple toga, long considered the garb of royalty, and on his head he often wore a wreath of laurel leaves (the Greek symbol of victory). He was called *Imperator*, a title that had traditionally meant "commander-in-chief" of the army, but in Caesar's case, it seemed to imply something more. (As we will see, Imperator came to mean the same thing as our modern word Emperor, which is the English translation of the Latin title.) Caesar was also honored with the title of *Pater Patriae* (Father of the Fatherland).

Caesar's Reforms

During the years of his rule, Caesar proved to be an astute politician and able administrator. Although he had more political power than any one of his predecessors, he maintained the structure of the Republican government. In order to strengthen public support for the government, he offered citizenship to large numbers of provincials. To reduce unemployment in Italy, he put large numbers of men to work on public construction projects: He ordered the redesign and enlargement of the Forum, the restoration of the Curia (the meeting place of the Senate) and the construction of the Basilica Julia (a law court).

Caesar gave the landless peasants an opportunity to return to farm work by offering them free land in many unsettled parts of the empire, and he promoted the founding of new colonies around the Mediterranean Sea. He set up government departments of transportation to improve traffic control on the crowded city streets of Italy and to supervise the upkeep of roads throughout the empire. He hired engineers to drain the marshes around Rome and to deepen the harbor of Ostia (now Rome's largest port). He appointed officials to supervise the public grain supply, and he made plans to build museums, to codify the civil law, and to revise the tax structure. Amidst all this activity, he also found time to write poetry and compose a Latin grammar book!

A public record of Caesar's proceedings was posted each day in the Forum: This was the world's first daily newspaper.

The Senators Become Alarmed

Caesar strengthened his own authority by reducing the role of the once-powerful Senate to that of an advisory council. At the same time, he diluted the influence of the wealthy within that body by increasing its numbers to nine hundred and extending membership to equestrians, provincials, the sons of slaves, and even the Gauls of northern Italy. This made the Senate a more representative body, but the patricians grew enraged as they saw their power waning. They also worried about Caesar's obvious love of power and his disregard for many long-held government practices. And they were furious when he had a law passed that enabled him to personally choose candidates for high office.

Caesar apparently did not fully appreciate the Roman reverence for tradition. When magistrates opposed him, he simply had them removed from office. He thought that he knew what was best for Rome, and although he turned down an offer of a crown three times, he was indeed king in every way but title. When he began to make plans to attack Parthia (in Asia) and appointed some of his political supporters to run the government while he was away, the opposition against him solidified. Caesar's time was running out.

The Conspiracy

In the fervent belief that that they were defending the old Republic, sixty men formed a conspiracy against Caesar. Actually, their mission was a futile one: They did not grasp the fact that a government designed to run a city-state was ill equipped to handle the problems of a huge empire. There was no way the Republic could be retained. It needed to be replaced by a new form of government.

Two of the leaders of the conspiracy, Gaius Cassius Longinus and Marcus Junius Brutus, were men Caesar considered his friends. On the eve of March 15 (the Ides of March) in 44 BC, the day when Caesar was scheduled to attend a meeting of the Senate, his wife Calpurnia had a nightmare about an evil force attacking her husband. She begged him not to attend the meeting. A soothsayer (fortune teller) named Spurinna also warned him to beware, but he dismissed the warnings as unfounded superstition and went to the Senate meeting. On his way there he spied Spurinna, and he confidently remarked, "The Ides of March have come" (meaning that all was well and there was nothing to fear). The soothsayer answered, "Ay, but not gone!"

The meeting took place in the Theater of Pompey, because the normal meeting room in the Curia was under repair. Suddenly, one of the senators grabbed Caesar's toga and pulled it off his shoulders: This was a signal for the attack. Within a few moments, Caesar was fatally wounded by twenty-three thrusts by the daggers of the conspirators. After his "friend" Brutus plunged in his knife, Caesar covered his face in his toga, staggered to the foot of a statue of Pompey, and fell dead. In Shakespeare's famous play, JULIUS CAESAR, the dying leader gasps, "Et tu, Brute?" (you, too, Brutus?). Whether or not Caesar uttered such words we shall never know, but thoughts of betrayal must have entered his mind as he fell to the floor. Interestingly enough, this traitorous Brutus was a direct descendant of the Brutus who had been one of the first two consuls of Rome.

Caesar's death, which was supposed to guarantee the survival of the old order, actually marked the end of the Republic. Roman history had arrived at a crucial turning point.

Octavian

In his will, Caesar left the bulk of his estate to his grand nephew, adopted son, and heir: Gaius Julius Caesar Octavianus or "Julius Caesar the Younger," known to us as Octavian. He also left to each citizen of Rome the sum of three hundred sesterces (a generous amount) as well as the use of his pleasant gardens along the Tiber. Octavian, a young man of eighteen, was studying in Greece at the time of the murder. Upon hearing the news of Caesar's assassination, he quickly returned to Rome. At first, no one took the slight and scholarly youth seriously.

Meanwhile, Marc Antony (Marcus Antonius), a talented general and Caesar's protegé and right-hand man, tried to restore order. In 43 BC Octavian proved his mettle by raising an army, and soon afterwards he joined forces with Antony and Marcus Aemilius Lepidus (Caesar's second in command) to form the Second Triumvirate. They ordered the execution of thousands of people suspected of opposing Caesar, including the great orator Cicero (his head and hands—the instruments of his persuasive speeches and writings—were nailed to the Rostra in the Forum). Brutus and Cassius fled with their armies to the east where they hoped to make a stand, but they were defeated by Antony and Octavian at Philippi in Macedonia. In the end, both conspirators committed suicide by running onto swords held by their slaves.

Soon after his death, Caesar was declared a god; this put Octavian in the politically advantageous position of being able to call himself the living son of a god.

Octavian and Antony now shared the leadership of the Roman Empire (Lepidus, a weaker personality, was pushed into the background by the other two men). Octavian was not really interested in military matters, but he was a gifted politician. Antony, on the other hand, was a good general, but he was rash and headstrong. So when Antony sailed east to deal with the uprisings in that part of the empire, Octavian remained in Italy.

Cleopatra Reenters the Scene

Cleopatra had taken Caesarion back to her homeland after Caesar's assassination and arranged for her Egyptian husband's murder. Then she began to look for ways to restore Egypt to its former glory. When Antony visited her, he became as infatuated as Caesar had once been, and Cleopatra saw in Antony and his legions the answer to her needs for building up her empire. The two became lovers, and together they began to plan the establishment of a vast kingdom made up of Egypt and the eastern Roman provinces. They had two children (twins, named Alexander and Cleopatra), and Antony became a second father to Caesarion.

Actium

Octavian was an ambitious man, and he relished the idea of becoming sole ruler of the empire. He was suspicious of Antony's liaison with Cleopatra, and he was concerned about the possibility of Caesarion someday claiming power in Rome (he was, after all, Caesar's only son). And he had other reasons to be angry: Antony had married Octavian's sister (Octavia) and then left her in Rome while he spent time in Egypt.

Octavian eventually launched a propaganda attack against Antony, suggesting that his rival wanted to create his own empire and make himself king. Of course, he presented himself as the defender of the traditions of the Roman Republic. He finally convinced the Senate to declare war on Cleopatra.

In 31 BC Octavian's fleet, commanded by his friend Marcus Vispanius Agrippa, easily defeated the ships of Cleopatra and Antony near Actium on the northwest coast of Greece. Soon afterwards Antony heard a rumor that Cleopatra had poisoned herself; in despair, he fell upon his sword. But the rumor was false! Cleopatra rushed to his side, but he died in her arms. A few days later she allowed herself to be bitten by an asp (a cobra snake). The asp was a royal symbol of ancient Egypt, and its bite brought a swift, painless death. Perhaps this dramatic ending was a fitting one for one of history's most fascinating love affairs.

Egypt became another province (an important acquisition, since Egypt was rich in grain), and Octavian was now sole ruler of a vast empire.

Questions:

1. Describe Caesar's boyhood.
2. List five adjectives that describe Caesar's personality.
3. How was Caesar related to Marius?
4. Explain how Caesar got along with plebeians as well as patricians.
5. What was the First Triumvirate?
6. Describe Caesar's consulship.
7. Why did Caesar go to Gaul?
8. How did Caesar defeat Vercingetorix?
9. Why did Caesar lead his soldiers into Rome?
10. Who was Caesarion?
11. List five of Caesar's reforms.
12. Why did the conspirators kill Caesar?
13. What was the Second Triumvirate?
14. How did Octavian and Antony differ in temperament?
15. What happened at Actium?

Ideas To Think About:

1. Patrician Roman men had three names. In the case of Caesar (Gaius Julius Caesar), Gaius was his first name,

Julius was the name of his clan, and Caesar was his family name. Caesar was in fact a descriptive word meaning "hairy" or "bright." Caesar set a fine example as a ruler, and after his death certain rulers referred to themselves as Caesar, although they were not necessarily of his family. Thus, the word Caesar came to signify ruler or monarch. In later years, the terms *czar* (tsar) and *kaiser*, Russian and German words meaning ruler, were derived from Caesar's family name.

Caesar's name pops up now and then in other areas as well. A Caesarean section is a medical term for the delivery of a baby through an incision in the mother's abdomen. According to legend, this is the method by which Caesar was born. And there is an island in the English Channel between Britain and France that the Romans called Caesarea. Over the years, the spelling and pronunciation of the island evolved until it became known as Jersey. The state of New Jersey (named for the island) thus derives from the famous Roman general!

2. After the Punic Wars, the Roman navy fell into disrepair and pirates roamed the Mediterranean unimpeded. When young Caesar was returning from his studies on the Greek island of Rhodes, he was kidnapped by some pirates and ransomed for a large sum of money. Although he was treated well, Caesar swore that he would seek revenge for his captivity (much to the amusement of the pirates!). After the ransom was paid and he was freed, Caesar collected a fleet of ships and returned to the scene of his kidnapping. He hunted down the pirates and had each of them crucified (hung from a wooden cross), mercifully cutting their throats to shorten the agony. Even as a youth, Caesar was not one to be pushed around!

3. Crassus increased his wealth in crafty ways. For example, contemporary observers wrote that he often set fire to the tenements in Rome. Then he would show up in front of a building and offer to buy the smoldering remains. The owner, wringing his hands and wishing to make the most of his loss, would willingly sell. At that point, Crassus would call out his fire brigade of slaves and quickly extinguish the blaze. In this way he became the landlord of a building for almost no cost! Needless to say, he put a minimal amount of money into the building to make it inhabitable.

4. The names of the months on our modern calendar date back to the Julian calendar. Januarius is named after the god Janus, Februarius is the month of purification, Martius is named for Mars, April means the time of opening, May is the time of growing, and June (named for Juno) is the time of ripening. The Roman year began in March (not January), and so the month after June was Quintilis (meaning the fifth month) and it, in turn, was followed by Sextilis (the sixth month). In the first century AD Quintilis was changed to July (in honor of Julius Caesar) and Sextilis was changed to August (after Octavian, later known as Augustus). Now, to continue the names of the months: September means seventh month, October means eighth month, November means ninth month, and December means tenth month. When January became the first month of the year, the Latin names of the last four months were retained. This explains why our ninth month is called the seventh month, our tenth month is called the eighth, and so on. Most people are completely unaware of this great inaccuracy!

Projects:

1. Caesar liked secret codes. While campaigning in Gaul, he wrote his messages in Greek, since they would be less likely to be understood if they were intercepted. In his missives to Rome, he used the following code: Each letter was replaced by the one coming three characters after it in the alphabet. Use Caesar's code to write a message to a classmate.

2. ASTERIX is a series of stories in a cartoon format about the Roman occupation of Gaul. The main character Asterix is based on the hero Vercingetorix. Although the books were first published in French, they are now available in English. They are a lot of fun to read, and they present many insights into the period when the Gauls tried to hold out against the Roman invaders. Find a copy of one of these books in your library and read it.

3. Two of Caesar's most formidable opponents in the Senate were Cato the Younger and Marcus Tullius Cicero. Find out more about these two men, and write a short report.

4. What is the meaning of the expression, "to cross the Rubicon?" Give a modern example illustrating this expression.

5. Read Antony's funeral oration in Shakespeare's play JULIUS CAESAR. Think about how Antony must have felt about the conspirators when he delivered it. Did he want his listeners to accept his words literally, or was he trying to imply something without actually saying it? Pretend you are Antony and read the oration to the class (as dramatically as you can).

Chapter X — Roads and Arches

Although the Romans were not particularly noted for their artistic talents, they were masters at technology (practical know-how). They experimented with the building techniques of the Etruscans, Greeks, and even the Egyptians, and they applied the knowledge they acquired in innovative ways. Their engineering skills, combined with their talent for organizing large numbers of people, enabled the Romans to construct impressive bridges, roads, and buildings, many of which are still standing today.

A Network of Straight Roads

The need to move troops quickly to a battlesite and to dispatch messages to campaigning generals motivated the Romans to build a system of well-paved roads. The shortest distance between two points is a straight line, and so the practical Roman engineers designed roads that were as straight as an arrow, bending only when there was no alternative on hilly terrain. By the first century AD, Rome had a network of excellent roads that enabled the legions to cover about twenty miles a day, while a mounted army messenger riding hard could cover over one hundred (changing mounts, of course). In ancient times, this was remarkable speed!

The Via Appia (Appian Way) is Europe's oldest paved road. It was built during the early Republic (312 BC) by the censor Appius Claudius Crassus to link Rome with Capua, the most important city in southern Italy. This is a distance of 234 miles. Do you remember how the newly constructed Appian Way enabled the legionaries to march into Campania in record time and defeat the Samnites? (See page 29 if you've forgotten.) The Via Flaminia was built soon after the completion of the Appian Way; it connected Rome with Rimini and became the major thoroughfare in northern Italy.

When the empire reached its greatest extent in the second century AD, 56,000 miles of military highways as well as 200,000 miles of secondary roads stretched in a vast network from Britain to the Euphrates River. It has been estimated that if the main roads were placed end to end, they would stretch around the equator two times! If Rome was the heart of the empire, the roads were its arteries.

Every mile along a road was marked by a tall milestone (a carved rock about the height of a man) which listed the distances to local towns. The Roman

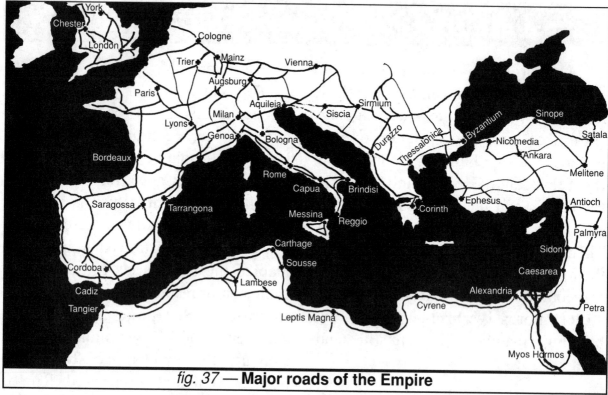

fig. 37 — **Major roads of the Empire**

mile was one thousand (*mille*) paces of a soldier or 1620 yards (a bit shorter than the modern mile). A central milestone in Rome was encased in bronze and marked in gold letters the distances to all major cities in the empire. This is the source of the familiar expression, "All roads lead to Rome."

Construction of the Roads

As we learned earlier, most of the roads were built by the army: The spade and ax carried by each of "Marius' mules" was used as much for road construction as for the setting up of a camp. Some of the heaviest labor was done by slaves, however. Of course, every legion had its own squad of surveyors and engineers.

The typical Roman road was twelve to fifteen feet wide (wide enough for two legions to pass one another or for three chariots to travel side by side).The Romans, as usual, had a set procedure for its construction. Once its outer boundaries were marked out, a shallow ditch was dug along each side and curbstones were set in them. Then the soldiers dug a trench four feet deep between the curbs and shoveled a layer of sand into it. After they had rolled the sand flat, they covered it with a layer of finely cut gravel. Once again they rolled the surface to make sure it was flat, preparing it for the third layer, which was a mixture of chunks of rock and concrete. As you can see, each layer of the road was more coarse then the one upon which it rested. The compact layers would provide a cushion for the heavy loads that were carried over them. Now the road was ready to be surfaced. The soldiers carefully arranged large paving stones which fit together so tightly that no mortar was necessary. The surface of the road was about three feet above the surface of the surrounding landscape, and it was cambered (high in the center and sloping on the sides) so that water would run off into ditches along the shoulders.

fig. 38 — **Cross-section of a road**

The surveyors would pick a spot on the horizon or a large tree in the distance and direct the road toward it; sometimes, if there was no natural object to serve as a focal point, a squad of soldiers was sent ahead to light a fire, and its smoke would serve as a marker. Devices called *gromae* were used to make sure that two roads intersected at right angles. A groma was simply a wooden cross mounted horizontally on a four-foot pole. From the end of each of the four parts of the cross was suspended a string with a small metal weight. When the four strings hung parallel to the pole, the surveyor knew that the pole was absolutely vertical (perpendicular to the ground). The intersecting road could be laid out according to the horizontal line of the cross.

fig. 39
A groma

Public Use of the Roads

When the roads were not being used by the army, merchants traveled along them from city to city, no doubt savoring this great opportunity to dramatically expand their markets. Indeed, the network of roads became a key to Rome's economic prosperity. Ordinary Roman citizens also took advantage of the fine system of roads, using different modes of transportation according to their station in life. A wealthy man might travel in a four-wheeled cart with a leather roof drawn by a team of horses, or he could simply ride horseback over shorter distances. However, it is important to realize that the carriages had no springs, and riding a horse without stirrups (they weren't invented until the Middle Ages!) was rather tiring. For very short distances, the well-to-do often traveled in litters carried on the shoulders of their slaves. Less affluent Romans drove two-wheeled carts pulled by oxen, or else they traveled on foot.

fig. 40 — **A farm cart moving along the highway**

Slow traffic was often obliged to follow a dirt path along the side of a road, making room for faster moving vehicles and mounted army messengers. Benches for weary travelers were placed at frequent intervals beside the roads, as were fountains and watering troughs where men and beasts could refresh themselves. Roman map makers often listed towns as well as convenient resting places along particular routes.

Road travel was usually limited to the daylight hours, since robbers were a dangerous menace at night. Inns were built alongside the highways, but they tended to be dirty and uncomfortable; most people tried to arrange to stay with friends in the area, or else they slept in their wagons or carriages.

Posting stations were placed at intervals of from six to sixteen miles for army messengers to rest or change horses, and every forty or fifty miles there was a fort (often at a strategic site where two roads joined). The towns that lay at important junctions became bustling cities: Marseilles, London and Naples date back to those early times.

The Romans built their roads to last, and indeed they have. Their system of highways was used by many cultures that flourished long after the Roman Empire had come to an end. Some of those ancient thoroughfares are still used today, while others have been transformed into modern highways.

The Use of the Arch

Since only a small portion of the Roman empire was open plains, the engineers had to design bridges to carry the roads across rivers and over deep mountain gorges. They discovered early on that the heavy weight of a long, stone bridge was most effectively supported by a series of arches.

An arch is basically a curved structure supported by two posts or columns. Although the Egyptians and the Greeks knew about the arch, they seldom used it in their buildings. The Etruscans experimented fleetingly with the concept, and then they passed on their knowledge of it to the Romans, who made the arch a key factor in their building projects.

The basic design of most ancient buildings was the post and lintel (two upright walls or rows of pillars supporting a horizontal roof). The pillars had to be placed fairly close together in order to support a heavy roof. The Romans discovered that an arch could support a very heavy weight while leaving a large, open space between its supporting columns. The possibilities for creating innovative new structures must have dazzled those early architects!

fig. 41 — **Post and lintel construction and the arch**

The Invention of Concrete

However, the arch could not be effectively used on a grand scale until the Romans invented a miraculous new building material: concrete. Improving upon the Egyptian formula for cement (a mixture of sand, lime and water), the Romans combined the volcanic sand (*pozzolana*) that was so prevalent in western Italy with lime and water and then added bits of stone rubble. This produced a substance that, when dry,

was stronger and yet lighter than cement. The invention of concrete enabled to Romans to accomplish feats of building and engineering that earlier peoples had never even dreamed about!

How To Build An Arch

Once the concept was understood, it was easy to build an arch. After two stone columns were constructed, the workers erected a semi-circular wooden framework (the skeleton of the arch) and placed it on the columns. Next, they laid an outer casing of precisely chiseled wedge-shaped blocks (voussoirs) along each outer edge, placing the keystones in the center last of all to lock all the other blocks in place. Then they removed the wooden framework and filled in the hollow space within the casing with concrete.

Sometimes the Romans built freestanding arches. The triumphal arch is a good example.

Roman Bridge Construction

A Roman bridge was basically a series of arches held up by large square posts that were built into the riverbed. One of the finest Roman bridges (the Alcantara) still rises 165 feet above a river in Spain. It is 655 feet long and is supported by six huge arches. When the bridge was completed, its architect chiseled the following inscription into the stone: "I have built a bridge that shall endure for centuries." And so it has!

The ingenious Romans even found a way for the laborers to construct the supporting piers of the bridges without having to work under water. First, a circle of long wooden piles (with pointed ends) was driven into the riverbed; then the piles were chained together and any gaps were filled in with clay. Once the water was pumped out, the workers could climb down and construct a pier of stone and concrete in the space within the piles. When the piers rose above the level of the water, they were connected with arches.

Aqueducts

As the Roman towns and cities grew, the local water supply was no longer adequate to supply the needs of the population. Therefore, the Roman engineers designed an extensive system of clay and lead pipes to bring in water from mountain lakes and streams. This system was called an *aqueduct*, which in Latin means "conveyor of water." Appius Claudius, the same man who built the Appian way, constructed the first Roman aqueduct; it transported water to Rome from the mountains fifteen miles east of the city. Of course, an essential part of the system of aqueducts was the arched bridge.

The aqueducts depended upon the force of gravity to deliver the water from the hills to the cities. The Roman engineers discovered that the pipes needed to descend at a rate of six inches every ninety-eight feet in order to maintain a steady downhill flow. If the slope was too great, the water pressure would increase until the pipes burst, and, of course, if it was too gentle, the water would not flow at all. The pipe lay just above the ground when the terrain was flat, tunneled through hills that lay in its path, and crossed rivers and gorges on arched bridges.

The construction of a bridge over the River Gardon in Nimes, France posed a particularly challenging problem. The river had cut a gorge 180 feet deep, and a bridge over it would have to be more than twice the height of the tallest arch the Romans could build without fear of collapse. The engineers resolved the problem by constructing a three-story bridge with one level of arches built upon the other! The two lower levels had the widest arches, each one spanning 82 feet. They were constructed of unmortared blocks weighing up to two tons each. The upper level, which carried the covered channel of water, was made up of groups of three arches over each of the larger lower ones. It was an elegant design. When it was completed, the bridge (called the

Pont du Gard) helped to supply twenty thousand tons of water a day to the city of Nimes from a source thirty miles away. The lowest tier was wide enough to bear both a paved road and the piers that supported the heavy upper levels.

fig. 42 — **A portion of the Pont du Gard**

The Romans built their bridges with rather primitive instruments, such as the leveling staff and plumb line. They used huge cranes to raise the large blocks of limestone and a system of hoists and pulleys to maneuver them into position.

At its height, the city of Rome had fourteen aqueducts delivering three hundred million gallons of water daily. Each aqueduct fed water into a large elevated water tower called a *castellum*. Three main pipes made of lead conduct-

ed the water from the tower to public fountains (for drinking water), public baths, the private homes of the wealthy and certain small businesses and mills. In times of water shortage, valves in the pipes were closed to cut off the supply to the private homes. The recipients of the water paid for the service according to the amount of water they received. Sometimes wealthy men bribed aqueduct builders to divert a stream of water to their private estates or to replace a narrow pipe with a wider one, thus doubling their water supply without increasing their fee!

The earliest aqueducts were designed so that the pipes were underground as much as possible to lessen the possibility of the water being poisoned by enemies. As Rome became a strong power, this fear lessened and most pipes were placed above ground. The aqueducts required constant inspection and repair, because the earth beneath them gradually settled and the stones frequently crumbled.

The Underground Sewers

The delivery of a huge supply of water to the city produced a new problem. How to get rid of the waste water? Long ago the Etruscans had built Rome's first sewer, a huge ditch called the Cloaca Maxima , but no one wanted a system of smelly channels running throughout the city! Returning to their drawing boards, the Roman engineers discovered that by lining up a series of arches they could produce a barrel-like roof (called a barrel vault). They used the new concept to create an underground network of covered channels. These sewers passed below the public lavatories to carry off the human waste. They were constantly flushed with the overflow from baths, fountains and water tanks. The (covered) Cloaca Maxima is still in use today.

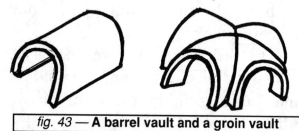

fig. 43 — **A barrel vault and a groin vault**

The Dome

As the architects continued to experiment with the arch, they found that when two barrel vaults intersected at right angles, they formed a cross (or groin) vault; this vault enabled them to create an airy, open space within a large public building. When they arranged a series of arches in a circle, an even larger space was opened up. They had invented the dome!

Construction of a dome was a simple process. After laying a circular foundation (about fifteen feet deep), the workers built a circle of columns spaced at regular intervals. Then they erected a circular wooden framework at the top of the columns. This was a giant mold divided into equal sections; the workers poured concrete into it, beginning at the lowest part. As they proceeded upward, they used ever finer grades of concrete until, near the top, they poured a cement blended with pumice (volcanic debris that is one of the lightest stones). In the very center they made an opening (the *occulus*) that admitted light and served as a compression ring to distribute the stress of the dome. The frame was removed after the concrete hardened.

The Pantheon is a Roman temple that houses the widest dome that was ever constructed using pre-industrial

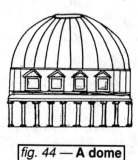

fig. 44 — **A dome**

fig. 45 — **The Pantheon**

technology. It rises 14 stories above the ground and has a diameter of 144 feet. The center of the dome is pierced by an oculus that is 30 feet in diameter.

Questions:

1. Why were the Roman roads first constructed?
2. What was the first Roman road called, and where was it built?
3. What was a milestone?
4. How was a Roman road constructed?
5. What are the advantages of the arch in building construction?
6. How do you make concrete?
7. What does the word "aqueduct" mean in Latin?
8. How did the Romans solve the problem of smelly open sewers?
9. How did the Romans construct a dome?

Ideas To Think About:

1. Long ago in England, the Saxons found the remains of some Roman roads cutting across the hilltops that bordered a stretch of flat farmland. They called the thoroughfare the "high way," and this is the origin of our modern word.

2. The Romans were the first people to use water power as a source of energy. They invented large wheels that were connected to long wooden shafts; when the water turned the wheels, the shafts activated the primitive machinery that made up history's first water mills.

3. Organizing workers was as important as planning the design of bridges and aqueducts, and the Romans excelled at this task. However, occasional problems did arise. In the second century AD, Nonius Datus was commissioned to plan the digging of a tunnel through a hill for an aqueduct. After surveying the site and drawing his plans, he was suddenly called away. When he returned, he discovered that each of the two crews of men who were supposed to dig from each side of the hill and meet at the middle had veered a bit to the right! Had Datus not immediately resolved the problem, there would have been two tunnels rather than one!

4. In the nineteenth century, Napoleon I of France considered himself an emperor of the Roman tradition. He was also a brilliant military leader. To celebrate his victory, he constructed his own arch of triumph in Paris. To this day, it is one of that city's most famous monuments.

Project:

1. Find out how modern roads are built and resurfaced. Compare the modern process to that of the Romans. Can you explain why the Roman roads lasted for millenia and modern roads need constant repair?

2. The arch is a self-supporting structure because each stone supports its neighbor, and the stress from the weight goes vertically into the ground. You can better understand this principle if you construct a small arch using wedge-shaped blocks of wood held together by bits of clay. Once the central block is put in place each block in the curve pushes against the one just below it. Since the pressure from one side of a block is cancelled out by that on the other, the stones support each another.

3. Consult the books in your classroom for an illustration of the Arch of Titus. Draw a detailed picture of what you see. Then find an illustration of the Arc de Triomphe in Paris (Napoleon's arch). How are the two arches similar, and how are they different? Write a short paragraph comparing and contrasting the two arches.

4. Be on the lookout for domes and arches. Make a list of ten examples of the use of domes and arches in a modern town or city. Then list five famous buildings whose design is based upon a dome or series of arches.

PART THREE — THE EMPIRE

CHAPTER XI - THE GOVERNMENT IS TRANSFORMED

Augustus

When Octavian defeated Marc Antony at Actium, he became the sole ruler of Rome. At the age of thirty-two, he commanded a gigantic empire that stretched entirely around the Mediterranean Sea (which was now called *Mare Nostrum* (our sea) by the arrogant Romans!). To symbolize the end of ninety long years of civil wars, he dramatically ordered the closing of the doors of the Temple of Janus (as we learned earlier, these doors were traditionally kept open whenever Rome was engaged in war).

Octavian well remembered how the Senate had reacted to Caesar's obvious love of power, and so he decided to play it safe. Using his considerable gifts as a politician, he charmed the Senate and the people of Rome into believing that he had restored the Republic. To demonstrate his lack of political ambition, he resigned from all offices. This ploy worked perfectly: The grateful Senate immediately rewarded such public spirit by offering him new titles that made him even more powerful than he had been before! To demonstrate his kinship to the people, he was called the *Princeps* ("First Citizen") of Rome. (Princeps is the source of our modern word "prince.") As First Citizen, Octavian acquired the authority of a tribune as well as the right to speak first on any matter that came up for discussion in the Senate. Thus, while appearing to be a representative of the common people, he ably gained the ability to propose and veto legislation. In other words, he now controlled the activities of Rome's most important bodies of government! Of course, Octavian publicly recognized the importance of the traditional government agencies, and official pronouncements always included the words "in the name of the Senate and the Roman people."

Octavian was eventually made proconsul of the provinces of Spain, Gaul and Syria, and, since most of the legions were stationed in those lands, he gained tremendous military power. Like Caesar, he was designated Imperator; in time, all Roman soldiers would swear allegiance to him personally.

Perhaps the highest honor the Senate bestowed upon Octavian was the title Augustus, which means "revered" or "majestic." Ever since, he has been known as Caesar Augustus or simply Augustus. We will refer to him in that way from now on. Although he carefully avoided the title of king, he was indeed a powerful monarch, and the Roman Empire officially began with his reign.

fig. 46 — **Augustus**
H.L. Pierce Fund — Courtesy, Museum of Fine Arts, Boston

Fortunately, Augustus had the best interests of Rome in mind as he skillfully achieved mastery over its citizens. The years of riots and fighting had turned the political structure into a shambles. For many it was a matter of survival in a dog-eat-dog world. Augustus reorganized the mess into an efficient bureaucracy that would function smoothly for centuries. He personally selected the candidates for all major elections, basing his choices on ability rather than political ties (a distinct improvement over the practices of the past), and he created a civil service of qualified magistrates from the equestrian class to deal with the day-to-day running of the empire. Augustus devised a system of taxes that was fair to most people, although his attempt to promote marriage in the patrician class (many people had been killed during the civil wars) by taxing unmarried people more heavily than married ones failed!

Do you remember how the provinces had been governed during the late Republic by former consuls, many of whom were unscrupulous men who exploited the local people by taxing them heavily and then pocketing the money? (If you've forgotten, see page 91.) Augustus eliminated this network of bribery and corruption by appointing able administrators to run the provincial governments and paying them handsomely for their services. He also provided means by which the people of the provinces could appeal to Rome if they felt they were being unjustly treated.

Augustus ruled for forty-one years. Despite the fact that he was an autocrat (he had unlimited powers), he was praised for his good sense, his political acumen, and his conscientious devotion to this work. In fact, the people considered him a hero for restoring the calm of Republican times.

The State of Roman Law

As long ago as the second century BC, the Roman magistrates had replaced the rather restrictive Twelve Tables of Law (see p. 23) with "formulas" of legal proceedings. A formula was a collection of data gathered from past cases relating to a specific issue, such as petty theft or unprovoked assault, with a suggested penalty for the offense. Each year, the praetors issued a list of new formulas that could be used in the law courts. This growing body of legal procedures enabled Roman law to respond to the needs of the expanding empire.

This process continued during the reign of Augustus. A standardized system of law that emphasized the rights of the individual was enforced in every city and province of the empire. Juries made up of seventy-five local citizens voted upon the innocence or guilt of the accused. Sometimes an accused person was defended by a lawyer (*advocatus*). Those found guilty were usually exiled from Rome; however, in cases involving violent crimes, the condemned criminal was given the choice of execution or suicide.

A City of Marble

With the restoration of stability and the establishment of an imperial government bureaucracy, the people of Rome could proudly refer to their city as "the capital of the world" (*caput mundi*). Augustus saw to it that Rome looked the part with a building program that was even more ambitious than Caesar's. In fact, so many mud-brick structures were replaced by impressive stone buildings (he built and restored eighty-two temples) that Augustus would later boast about how he had "found a city of bricks and left it a city of marble."

fig. 47 — **A Roman temple**

Augustus helped the poor by creating jobs on the huge construction projects. He set up a combined police force and fire brigade (the *vigiles*) to protect the city, and he doubled the water supply.

After the death of Lepidus in 12 BC, Augustus became pontifex maximus. He tried to stimulate Roman patriotism by restoring the old gods (worship had fallen off considerably) and he rebuilt the temple of Jupiter. He also built a temple to the deified Julius Caesar on the spot where his great uncle's body had been cremated. Statues of the Princeps were set up at all military headquarters and in most provincial towns. The people of the eastern provinces eventually began to worship Augustus as a living god, and an organization of priests called the Augustales attracted large numbers of followers throughout many Italian cities.

Trade

Although the Romans built an extraordinary network of well-paved roads, the transport of products along them was expensive and relatively slow. For this reason, many merchants sent their wares to foreign ports by ship. The Romans never really liked the sea (many were convinced that it was inhabited by terrible monsters!), but for economic purposes, they constructed a number of rather seaworthy cargo ships. Ostia, the port at the mouth of the Tiber, flourished as a bustling center of trade.

The Roman ships hugged the coast as much as they could without crashing into the rocks, and they never ventured out of port during bad weather. Setting sail in winter was completely out of the question. The ships were protected from pirates by a revamped Roman navy.

Large quantities of Italian wine and olive oil were transported in clay vessels called *amphorae*. The shape of these vessels allowed them to be tightly packed together in the hold of a ship. In fact, seamen measured a ship's capacity in amphorae.

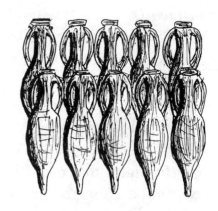

fig. 48 — **Amphorae**

Goods and products were sent to Rome from all parts of the empire. Egypt supplied nearly all of the city's wheat supply; huge freighters transported thousands of linen sacks of grain to Ostia on a weekly basis. Other parts of Africa provided the wild animals that were torn apart in the public spectacles. Gaul was known for its fine wine, cloth, pottery and silver, while Greece specialized in olive oil, salt, honey, wine, marble, and sculpture. Roman ships sailed to Britain for tin, hides, lead, and wool, and they even sailed to India (for cotton). Meanwhile, long camel trains still followed the overland route to deliver such luxury items as silk, jewels, and spices from China.

The Roman currency was based upon a silver coin called a *denarius*. Originally, one denarius was the value of ten asses (donkeys); in fact, the word "denarius" literally means "ten asses." An *aureus* was a gold coin that was worth twenty-five denarii. Beginning with Julius Caesar, the head of the reigning ruler was always depicted on one side of every Roman coin.

Military Reforms

Augustus was concerned about his own safety, and so he created an elite army unit, the Praetorian Guard, to protect himself and his family. It was commanded by two prefects whom he personally appointed. The Guard kept watch over the imperial palace and government buildings, and it accompanied Augustus into battle. It was stationed in a single camp on the outskirts of Rome. Over the years, membership in the Guard became a much sought-after position among ambitious legionaries. This was because it offered higher pay, better conditions and greater status than the ordinary legions, and it

required a shorter term of duty. Eventually, the Guard grew from 4,500 to nearly 10,000 men, and it became an extraordinarily powerful military tool in the hands of the Roman emperor. As we will see, it could also turn against him.

Because it was incredibly expensive to pay the salaries of the large numbers of troops making up the army as well as their retirement bonuses, Augustus disbanded all but twenty-five of his legions. At the same time, he recruited replacement troops from the provinces, promising them citizenship and a bonus if they served for twenty years. Most of the soldiers were now stationed permanently along the borders, where their primary duty was to keep out marauding barbarian tribesmen.

Under Augustus, several legions conquered the European regions to the northeast (modern Switzerland and Austria as well as parts of Hungary and the Balkans), thereby advancing the Roman frontier to the Danube and Rhine Rivers. The Princeps experienced his one great military disappointment in eastern Germany. After a twenty-year campaign to absorb the relatively small territory between the Rhine and the Elbe River into his empire, he sent three legions under the command of Quintilius Varus to finish off the job. Varus was not a brilliant general (to say the least!), and he was easily lured into a trap set by

Arminius, a German leader who had learned about military strategy when he was a Roman commander. The legions were surrounded and attacked in a swampy forest: Nearly every man was killed or captured, and Varus committed suicide. Eastern Germany was permanently lost to the Romans. Long after this massacre, Augustus allegedly wandered through his palace in the middle of the night crying out, "Varus, Varus, give me back my legions!"

The Pax Romana

Under the leadership of Augustus, the Roman Empire entered a period of peace and prosperity known as the *Pax Romana* (the Roman Peace). It lasted about two hundred years (27 BC-AD 180). This was the first time in history that all the lands surrounding the Mediterranean Sea were at peace and united under a single government. During these years, the highly efficient Roman bureaucracy and the vast network of roads led to the development of many commercial centers; new cities were built in the provinces that were modeled on those in Italy, each with a central Forum, theaters, marble temples, public baths, columned government buildings, paved roads, aqueducts and underground sewers. People throughout the empire could enjoy peace of mind, secure in the knowledge that their way of life was protected by the most invincible army in the world.

A Sprawling Empire

The Roman Empire now covered two million square miles on three continents, an area two thirds as large as the United States. It stretched from Spain on the west to Syria on the east, from the Rhine and Danube Rivers on the north to Egypt and the Sahara on the south. It was the greatest empire the world had ever known, with a frontier extending for six thousand miles. It was so vast, in fact, that ten weeks were required to send a message from the eastern boundary to the westernmost point!

The empire was made up of a great diversity of peoples. However, there was a fundamental difference between the eastern and western regions. The eastern provinces had adopted the Greek culture several centuries earlier during the reign of Alexander the Great, and they were considerably more civilized than the more primitive areas of Gaul, Spain, and northwestern Africa. Alexandria in Egypt and Antioch in Syria were prosperous cities that rivaled Rome in wealth and population. Yet, all of the millions of people living around Mare Nostrum were bound together by Roman law and Roman government. Latin was spoken throughout the

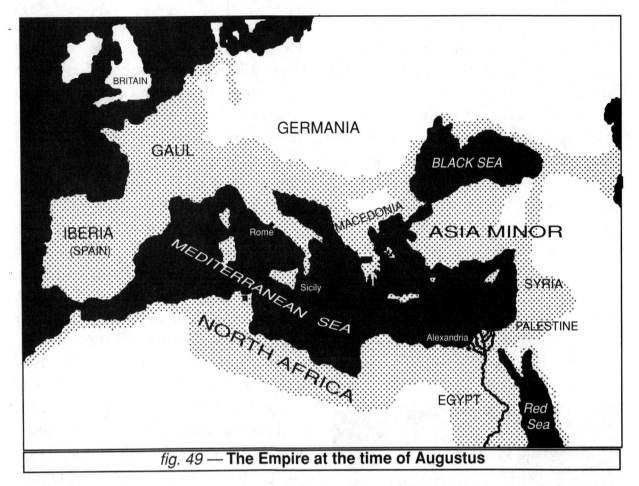

fig. 49 — **The Empire at the time of Augustus**

provinces, and all traders used a single currency (the denarius).

By the middle of the first century AD the empire had expanded nearly as far as it could, for it was now bounded by seas, wasteland and areas populated by ferocious barbarians. Its population was nearly eighty million people.

The Successors of Augustus

Augustus died peacefully in Campania in AD 14. Upon his death he was officially proclaimed a god. The government bureaucracy he had created would function efficiently for generations, in spite of a number of incompetent leaders.

For the next fifty-four years, Rome was ruled by emperors who were related to Caesar or were adopted into his family; they are known as the Julio-Claudian Emperors. The title "Imperator" now clearly meant "ruler of the empire."

Augustus was succeeded by Tiberius (Tiberius Claudius Nero), his aging stepson (Tiberius was fifty-five). The new emperor was granted for life the powers Augustus had held. He accepted his position with little enthusiasm, glumly acknowledging that he was the only possible candidate (all of Augustus' closest heirs had died). However, he was an able general, and he worked closely with the Senate. Tiberius was a distrustful man (given the mysterious deaths of some of his relatives he had reason to be!), and he imposed the death penalty on anyone who even muttered an unkind word about himself or his family. He put his faith in only one man: an ambitious prefect of the Praetorian Guard named Sejanus. Unfortunately, Sejanus proved to be a self-seeking, manipulative opportunist. Tiberius eventually became so tired and disen-chanted with the demands of political life that he withdrew to the island of Capri. He lived there for the last eleven years of his reign, ruling "long distance." As for Sejanus, he reveled in the powers Tiberius had given him until he was accused of poisoning the emperor's son, Drusus. He was tried and executed in AD 31.

When Tiberius died, the senators were relieved that they would once again have an emperor living in Rome. Their contentment was short-lived, however, for Tiberius had named as heir his nephew Gaius (Gaius Caesar Augustus Germanicus), a very poor choice indeed. As a child, Gaius had enjoyed visiting army camps, where the soldiers treated him as a sort of mascot and gave him a small pair of army boots (caligae) to wear. This is how he got the nickname Caligula ("Little Boots"), and he has been known by it ever since.

At first Caligula seemed to be a model ruler, but before long he began acting very strangely. Most historians believe that he was insane. He made his horse Incitatus a consul (the animal was kept in a marble stall and covered with a purple blanket). He later assembled an army near the English Channel with the expressed intention of invading Britain and then ordered the men to gather seashells!

Beginning with Caesar, many

fig. 50 — Tiberius as a young man
Edwin E. Jack Fund Courtesy, Museum of Fine Arts, Boston

emperors were considered gods after they died, and temples were built in their honor. Caligula, however, wanted to be worshiped while he was still alive! He had the heads of Greek statues removed and replaced with ones resembling himself. These were put in public places around Rome. He also had a temple built in his own honor, and every day the golden life-sized statue that stood within it was dressed in garments exactly matching those the Emperor had put on that morning. Caligula would sometimes sit in the temple of Castor and Pollux (sons of Jupiter) between the statues of the twins, awaiting adoration by the priests. And he claimed to have conversations with Jupiter himself!

Caligula was also very cruel, and it is no surprise that he met with an early (and violent) death: After four years of rule, he was assassinated by the Praetorian Guard. He was twenty-nine years old. Some scholars have speculated that Caligula's madness was caused by lead poisoning in his drinking water (remember, the pipes were lined with lead).

Caligula's successor was his uncle Claudius (Tiberius Claudius Caesar Augustus Germanicus), an intelligent and scholarly man. As a child, Claudius had been crippled (perhaps by polio), and he stuttered and twitched badly; Augustus purposefully kept him out of public view. After Caligula was assassinated, Claudius was found hiding behind a curtain in the palace. The Guard supposedly selected him to be Emperor as a joke! However, Claudius was a good administrator, and he ruled Rome for thirteen years with considerable success. He added two new provinces to the empire: Mauretania in Africa and Thrace (modern Bulgaria). He later succeeded where Caesar had failed: He conquered Britain. He even had time to complete a multi-volume history of the Etruscan people. Alas, poor Claudius was less successful in dealing with women, and he was poisoned by a mushroom dish prepared by his fourth wife, his niece Agrippina. She was a scheming, ambitious woman who did poor Claudius in once she had persuaded him to adopt her son Nero as his heir.

Nero (Nero Claudius Caesar) was an eccentric, to say the least! He was only a teenager when he found himself ruler of Rome. He shocked the patricians by personally taking part in musical and theatrical contests (the upper class considered actors a socially inferior lot). He sang and recited poetry (poorly) when he should have been concerned about the barbarians who were invading from the north. He also contrived to murder Britannicus (Claudius' son and the rightful heir to the throne), his mother

Agrippinna, and his wife Octavia.

During Nero's reign, twenty-five acres of land in the heart of Rome were destroyed by a terrible fire. According to legend (there are so many stories about Rome's more colorful emperors!), as the flames lit up the evening sky the Emperor played his lyre and sang about the fall of Troy. Afterwards, he ordered the construction of a huge complex of magnificent buildings intended solely for his private entertainment at the site of the fire. The main structure was called the Golden House, because its outer walls were adorned with gold (and mother of pearl). The buildings were surrounded by forests, parks, and pavilions, as well as a large artificial lake. Near the entrance to the complex stood a colossal (120 foot high) gilded bronze statue of Nero wearing the crown of Apollo. When the project was completed, Nero remarked, "At last I can begin to live like a human being!" When certain dubious citizens suggested that Nero had purposely started the fire to clear space for his grandiose facilities, he retorted that the Christians were obviously to blame for the conflagration, since the flames had spared their living quarters (we'll learn more about the Christians in a later chapter).

Nero toured Greece and participated in many local festivals there. Of course, he won the first prize in every competition (after all, he *was* the Emperor!), and he brought home over eighteen thousand gold crowns! He also raced chariots in the Circus Maximus. His outrageous behavior offended practically everyone, and conspiracies abounded. When he learned that his armies had rebelled against him, Nero committed suicide. As he lay dying, he sighed that the unlucky Romans were losing a great poet. Few agreed!

The Flavians

After the Julio-Claudian Emperors, a series of army generals seized power. In AD 69, Vespasian (Titus Flavius Vespasianus) restored peace and established a new dynasty known as the Flavians. Rome was able to recover from the excesses of Nero's reign, and many of the unemployed were put to work in a program of public works. Vespasian ordered the rebuilding of the temple of Jupiter Optimus Maximus, and under his authority construction began on a huge amphitheater known as the Colosseum. When Vespasian died, he joined the ranks of those deceased emperors who were deified (Caesar, Augustus, and Claudius). In fact, his dying words were, "Oh dear, I'm afraid I'm becoming a god!"

Vespasian's son Titus was a good ruler. When he died (from a plague), he, too, was worshiped as a god. Unfortu-

*fig. 51 — **Domitian** — Benjamin Pierce Cheney Donation, Courtesy, Museum of Fine Arts, Boston*

The Five Good Emperors

After a short interval, a new dynasty of emperors called the Antonines was established. They are also known as the Five Good Emperors, since they were all able, hard-working and efficient rulers. They reigned for the rest of the Pax Romana, and during that time Rome experienced its greatest prosperity.

The first of the Antonines was a rather elderly lawyer named Nerva; after reestablishing peace and restoring the Senate to an advisory position, he died. He was followed by his adopted heir Trajan (Marcus Ulpius Trajanus), a Spaniard who was thus the first non-Italian ruler of Rome. Trajan added the Asian territories of Dacia, Armenia and Mesopotamia to the Roman Empire, pushing the borders to their greatest limit. There were now forty-three provinces covering a million and three-quarters square miles.

Trajan erected a huge column (132 feet high) in the center of Rome to commemorate his victory over the Dacians. (To this day the land of the Dacians bears the name of their conquerors: Romania.) Trajan's Column is decorated with a great spiral relief sculpture that tells the story of his campaign. Hundreds of carved figures make up an intricate panorama that coils from the bottom to the top of the

nately, Domitian (the son and successor of Titus) was mentally unstable, and he was a tyrannical ruler. When he was assassinated (in a plot headed by his wife and servants and backed by the senators), the question of his deification never came up! Every trace of him was destroyed (his statues were defaced and the inscriptions erased). The pattern emerging of the destinies of Roman rulers was a grim one. Of the first ten emperors, seven had either been murdered or had committed suicide.

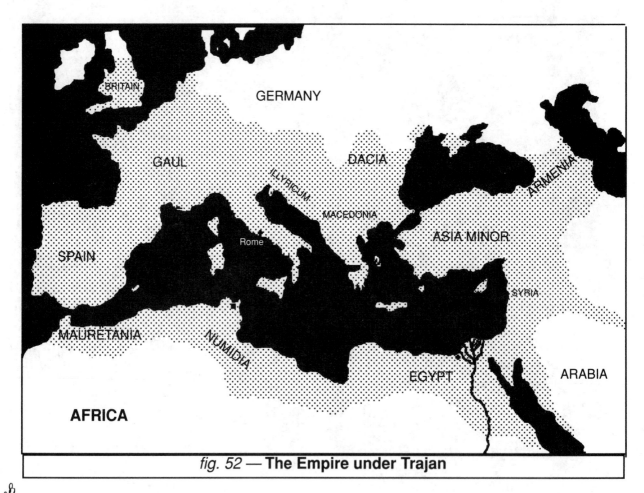

fig. 52 — **The Empire under Trajan**

column. The column provides a fascinating and detailed record of the legions of Imperial Rome. Originally, a statue of Trajan stood at the top of the column, but this has been replaced by one of St. Peter.

The booty from his war with the Dacians enabled Trajan to undertake a program of public works on a grand scale, including the construction of the city's largest and most elaborate public bath facilities on the site of Nero's Golden House. When he died, his ashes were placed within the pedestal of his column, making him the only man to be legally buried inside the city gates.

Trajan was succeeded in 117 A.D. by Hadrian (Publius Aelius Hadrianus), a practical man who felt that the army was being stretched beyond its ability to function. His solution was to return the governing of Armenia and Mesopotamia to the local people. Hadrian spent most of his reign traveling around the empire—visiting his legions and talking with his magistrates. In fact, he traveled more widely than any ruler since

fig. 53 — **Trajan's column**

Augustus. Hadrian ordered the construction of a seventy-five-mile wall across northern Britain stretching from sea to sea to keep out the barbaric Picts of Scotland. Major sections of this wall (known as Hadrian's Wall) still remain.

Hadrian had a keen intellect and an appreciation of art. He studied geometry and Greek philosophy, and he played the flute quite well. He summoned many of the best Greek artists to Rome, and he ordered the construction of the domed Pantheon (see page 110). He admired the lines of the ancient obelisks (tall decorated columns) of Egypt, and so he imported many of them to his capital city. In fact, most of the surviving Egyptian obelisks can be found in modern Rome.

Antoninus Pius was the fourth Good Emperor. During his reign, Rome experienced a long period of peace and prosperity. Yet, it was mostly the rich and powerful who were able to profit from the good times, and the needs of the poor were neglected. Furthermore, no one seemed to notice the barbarians who were gathering in increasing numbers along the frontier.

Marcus Aurelius was the last and the greatest of the Five Good Emperors. He was a humble man, an intellectual (he wrote many long, philosophical essays called THE MEDITATIONS), and he was an army general only by

necessity. He devoted most of his time to pushing back the hordes of German barbarians who were threatening the empire's northern border (finally, someone had noticed!). He needed more money to support his legions, so he reluctantly raised taxes. Aurelius felt rather torn between the need to defend his empire and the limitations of his resources. When some of his soldiers demanded a reward after a victory, he told them he would have to "wring it from the blood of their parents and kinsmen!" Because many Roman farmers were killed in the wars along the borders, Aurelius encouraged numbers of Germanic barbarians to settle on the Roman soil to help defend the border from future invaders. This policy would produce problems in future years.

Aurelius's death in 180 AD marks the end of the Pax Romana. He named as his heir an unworthy son, Commodus, who proved to be a cruel despot. He believed himself to be the incarnation of the superhero Hercules, and his greatest ambition was to be a gladiator in Rome's amphitheater (which he was on nearly one thousand occasions!). When Commodus was strangled in his bathtub in 192, Rome once again slipped into a state of civil war.

Questions:

1. What does Mare Nostrum mean?
2. How did Octavian trick the Senate into giving him a great deal of power?
3. How did Augustus improve the governing of the provinces?
4. What improvements did he make in the city of Rome?
5. Who was Varus and why did Augustus often think about him?
6. What is the meaning of the words Pax Romanus?
7. Name the Julio-Claudian emperors.
8. Describe Nero.
9. Name five good things that were accomplished by the Five Good Emperors.

Ideas to Think About:

1. Augustus lived in a rather modest house on the Palatine Hill, the district traditionally inhabited by the rich. Later emperors (beginning with Tiberius) built grander houses there. Our word "palace" comes from the Latin word for the Palatine residence of the emperor.

2. Roman citizens sometimes appealed to Augustus for unusual reasons. One particular incident gives us a good idea of the practical nature (and perhaps the sense of humor) of the Emperor. The farmers of the Balaeric Islands asked Augustus for permission to abandon their homes. They complained that rabbits were eating everything in sight, and that they would soon be facing famine. Augustus responded by sending them a shipload of ferrets (small rodent-like animals that love to eat rabbits)!

3. The early Latins had known about the dangers of swamps. Tarquin the Proud drained the swamps of the Tiber surrounding Rome because of the *mal aria* (bad air) that caused a disease (malaria). As we have seen, later sewage systems took the rain water and waste out of the city. During the Empire, the government employed inspectors to make certain that there was clean water for public baths and that the food in the market was not contaminated. A public health service was set up for the poor (the rich had their own doctors) and the first hospital was built. (See page 56, # 2)

4. When Nero was Emperor, he had the Greek Olympic Games postponed for two years (until AD 67) so that he could compete in the chariot race. When the event took place, Nero fell from his chariot and the race had to be stopped while he remounted. Even then, he failed to finish the race. However, he was named the winner, the logic being that *if* he had finished he would have won!

5. Most of Rome's important emperors lived during the Pax Romana. Here is a list of them to help you keep their order straight.

The Julio-Claudians: Augustus, Tiberius, Caligula, Claudius, Nero

The Antonines (the Five Good emperors): Nerva, Trajan, Hadrian, Antoninus Pius, Marcus Aurelius

Projects:

1. There were two provinces that were never truly content being a part of the Roman Empire: Egypt and Judea. In Egypt, the peasants were greatly exploited to produce the huge amounts of wheat that were needed to feed the masses in Rome. Episodes of civil disobedience became numerous during the reign of Nero. In Judea, the Romans never could establish a compromise with the Jewish religious customs and political traditions. A particularly tragic event occurred on the mountain top fortress of Masada when a group of Jewish rebels chose self-inflicted death over surrender to the Romans. The defense of Masada has become a symbol for modern Israel. Learn about the circumstances of this rebellion and write a short report.

2. Find out the derivation of the word "barbarian." (Hint: It was coined by the ancient Greeks.) How has the meaning of the word changed since those early times?

3. Choose one of the emperors (not counting Augustus) you have read about in this chapter. Find out more about him and write a short report. Be sure to explain why you think he was (or wasn't) a great ruler.

4. Marcus Aurelius adopted the Greek philosophy known as Stoicism. He believed that its principles perfectly fit the Roman character. Find out about Stoicism. Then write a short report explaining in what ways it seems to reflect the traditional Roman view of life.

5. I, CLAUDIUS is a fascinating book by Robert Graves that recounts the colorful history of the family of Augustus, ending with the death of Claudius. There is also an excellent series produced by the BBC for public television; videos are available. Read several chapters of the book (you'll probably want to read the whole thing) or view some of the segments of the film series. (These are excellent materials for small group or class discussions.)

CHAPTER XII — ARTS AND ENTERTAINMENT

The City

In the first century AD the city of Rome had about one million inhabitants and covered almost eight square miles. It was the largest city in the ancient world. Slaves made up two fifths of Rome's population at this time, and, despite public works projects initiated by Augustus, a sizeable number of citizens remained out of work. To pacify the idle masses, Augustus stepped up the government program of bread and circuses. One hundred and fifty-nine days (one third of the year) were declared public holidays; at these times, all businesses were closed and lavish spectacles were presented.

Augustus' impressive building program transformed Rome into the most majestic city in the ancient world. New marble-faced buildings went up all over the city—basilica (law courts) theaters, baths, and two libraries (one on the Palatine Hill and the other in the Campus Martius). Among the new structures, surely the most impressive were the temples. As we have learned, the Roman architects sited their temples on tall stone pedestals in open spaces so that they could be seen and admired from a distance (a design dating back to the Etruscans). Among the many temples Augustus had built was one that commemorated his victory at Philippi. Dedicated to Mars, it was filled with great treasures of art seized at the time of his campaign. He also dedicated a splendid temple on the Palatine Hill to Apollo, who had helped him defeat Antony's patron god Neptune at the sea battle near Actium.

The Colosseum

The Colosseum was Rome's largest amphitheater. As mentioned earlier, it was built between 69 and 80 AD by the emperors Titus and Vespasian. Since the site chosen for the arena was Nero's artificial lake, the first task in its construction was to install a drainage system of stone sewers to divert the water to the Tiber. Once the land was drained, the workers used stone, concrete and marble to erect a structure of awesome dimensions: Its oval seating area of 617 feet by 513 feet enclosed an arena that was 282 feet by 177 feet. The design of the building was similar to our modern sports stadiums. It rose four stories (187 feet) and contained many broad passages and stairways, which enabled an audience of 50,000 (45,000 seated and 5,000 standing) to reach the numbered seats with ease.

At the top of the amphitheater was an enclosed gallery that was reserved for women and the poor; below that was another gallery for slaves and foreigners. What does this tell you about the status of Roman women? Beneath the two galleries were tiers of marble seats for middle class citizens. The front rows in the amphitheater were reserved for wealthy businessmen. There were special boxes for senators, priests, magistrates, Vestal Virgins, and members of the Emperor's family.

The inner corridors of the Colosseum had gilded walls, painted ceilings and stone mosaic floors. There were broad passageways (appropriately called *vomitoria*!) that led to seventy-six exits (each marked with a number), so that the crowd could leave quickly and in an orderly manner. There were four other exits, two for the Emperor and two for the gladiators. One of the gladiator exits was named the *Libitina* (after the goddess of death); it was through its gates that the corpses of the losers were carried out!

The outer walls of the Colosseum were a series of arches interspersed with Greek columns. The placement of the columns dramatically reflects the successive eras of Greek architecture: On the ground floor are Doric columns (the earliest style), on the second story are Ionic columns (a later style), and on the third story are Corinthian columns (the style produced toward the end of the classical Greek civilization). Statues stood in arches between the columns. On the fourth level of the building there was an enormous canvas awning (the *velarium*); it was suspended by hundreds of cables, and it shielded the spectators from the rain or the hot summer sun.

fig 54 — **Ruins of the Colosseum**

The Colosseum became a setting for the bloody gladiator contests described in an earlier chapter. It was a tradition that the entering gladiators, wearing gold and purple cloaks, marched across the arena to the Emperor's box and shouted, "Hail Emperor, we who are about to die salute you." Although most gladiators were slaves, there were a few citizens who fought in the arena purely for the excitement and fame it offered them. (And, you will remember, the Emperor Commodus loved participating in the contests, although in his case, the outcome must have been rigged!) The

Romans admired the courage and endurance of the gladiators, and they always hoped for a good fight. The crowd eagerly shouted in unison "*Jugula*!" when one gladiator lost his footing or was knocked to the ground. A rough translation is "go for the jugular!"

We learned earlier that the gladiator fights had their origins in the funeral rites of the Etruscans. Although these events had lost most of their religious significance by the time of the Empire, there were a few lingering references to the ceremonies of the past. For example, individual contests were known as *munera* (offerings), and a special attendant who whacked a fallen gladiator on the head to be sure he was dead was dressed as Charon (the ferryman in the Underworld).

The Colosseum was also the setting for cruel animal fights. Cages holding the beasts were located below the heavy wooden planks of the arena. As in Republican times, the animals were starved for three days so that they would be ravenous; just before a fight, they were passed up to the floor of the arena on special counterbalanced elevators. As the doors opened, they ran out to hunt or be hunted by trained animal fighters (*bestiaris*). A catwalk ran around the upper rim of the Colosseum. Archers were stationed there to shoot any animal that was lucky enough to elude its hunter. When the arena was covered with carcasses, attendants clad as demons entered from side doors, dug hooks into the bodies, and then dragged them out!

The Romans celebrated the opening of the Colosseum with a hundred days of bloody spectacles. In one day, five thousand exotic animals (bears, tigers, elephants, buffalo, rhinos, and leopards) were slaughtered. This insatiable desire for bloodshed led to the disappearance of many animal species, such as the lion of Mesopotamia, the elephant of North Africa, and the hippopotamus of Nubia.

On some occasions, the planks of the floor were removed and the entire arena was flooded by an underground canal system. Then galleys manned by great numbers of slaves reenacted famous naval battles. The losers drowned! These water spectacles were called *naumachia*. The very first one was presented nearly a century earlier by Julius Caesar. He had a huge trench dug in the Campus Martius and filled with water from the Tiber for the occasion.

Numerous other events took place in the Colosseum: archery contests, boxing matches, and fights between charioteers. There were even lady sword fighters! Many of these contests were accompanied by background music that was played on trumpets and hydraulic organs. The spectacles became even more lavish and costly during the Pax Romana. Trajan once sponsored a festival that lasted 117 days and involved ten thousand gladiators!

Originally called the Flavian Amphitheater, the Colosseum acquired its more familiar name because it stood next to the colossal statue of Nero. Unfortunately, the statue was demolished long ago. But despite the damage sustained during several earthquakes (and the removal of much of the original masonry in medieval times), the Colosseum itself remains the largest surviving building of ancient Rome.

A Day At The Circus

The Circus Maximus was a huge racetrack (hippodrome) built between the Aventine and Palatine Hills. The original track was laid out in Etruscan times, but the stadium was expanded several times until it held nearly 250,000 spectators (a quarter of Rome's population). The Circus was used for races as well as animal fights until the Colosseum was built. In the late fourth century, it was enlarged a final time to hold 350,000 people.

At the entrance to the Circus were twelve arches. They represented the twelve months of the year (and the signs of the Zodiac). Vendors stood by the entrances with their pushcarts selling wine, bread, fruit, and cheese, just as modern hawkers sell pretzels and hot-dogs to fans in front of baseball stadiums.

As was the case with the Colosseum, admission to the Circus was free. After all, the public spectacles were largely intended to entertain people who had no money. But, unlike Republican days, when politicians paid for the events (in hopes of acquiring votes), the government now subsidized them.

Before the races began, the crowd was treated to a ritual procession of priests and magistrates. These distinguished men were followed by musicians, dancers and clowns. Perhaps this is the origin of our modern circus!

There were usually about twenty-four races held at the Circus in one day. The Emperor (or presiding magistrate) started a race by dropping a white cloth. Other similar cloths were distributed to the audience as they took their seats; the fans waved them wildly as they watched the competitions. The horse-drawn chariots burst out of starting gates that opened simultaneously and raced around the oval track seven laps (about five miles), often colliding at the hairpin turns as the crowd roared with delight. (The Romans called these crashes "shipwrecks!") Frequently, a charioteer rounded the turns on one wheel in an effort to gain extra seconds. Fouling (cutting off opponents) was permitted and even considered part of the sport! The metal rims of the chariot wheels got so hot that slaves standing on the track had to douse them with buckets of water; otherwise, the sparks might have set the wooden chariots on fire. The completion of each lap was indicated by the change in position of one of seven large wooden eggs (or dolphins) posted high in the center of the course. The victor of a race won a crown as well as a purse of gold. The Emperor Nero often raced at the Circus, when he wasn't busy reciting his poetry!

fig. 55 — **A racing chariot and horses**

The Romans were avid gamblers, and they bet heavily on the horses, choosing the colors of the four racing stables (green, red, blue, and white). The colors represented the four elements: earth, fire, water and air. The Emperor always backed one color, the reds for example, and to bet against that color was often considered a sign of dissatisfaction with the government. The horses had strands of pearls braided into their manes and ribbons of their stable's colors woven into their tails. Some harnesses were studded with medallions and colorful stones.

A charioteer named Gaius Apuleius Diocles (a Spaniard) had 4,257 starts and won 1,462 victories. He retired at the age of forty-two after earning the equivalent of over $1 million for the red stable over a period of twenty-four years. Nine of his horses won 100 times, and one horse was a 200-time winner.

Needless to say, Diocles was the hero of every other charioteer.

The Public Baths

Because the working day ended around noon, most Romans spent nearly every afternoon at the public baths (*thermae*). By the time of the Empire, the simple bath house had expanded into a rather complex facility that offered a variety of activities. Let's follow the daily routine of a typical Roman bather (we'll call him Marcus).

Upon entering the complex, Marcus removes his clothes in a dressing room and then moves on to the exercise area. There he has the choice of playing ball, wrestling, or perhaps doing some calisthenics. Then on to the hot room (the *sudatorium*), a sort of sauna. The purpose of this room is to make a person sweat in order to clean out his skin pores. A furnace stoked by slaves in the basement heats the air, which is then circulated under the floor and through ducts within the walls. This is called a *hypocaust* ("heat underneath") system, and it was one of the Romans' most practical inventions. Marcus wears wooden sandals in the sudatorium to protect his feet on the hot floor. He sprinkles his sweating body with oil (soap was unknown) and then scrapes it off with a metal instrument called a strigil (a Greek invention).

The next step is to ease into the *caldarium* (the hot pool). The water has been heated in huge tanks over the basement furnace and pumped through lead pipes. After a short while, Marcus has had enough of the hot water, so he moves on to the warm pool (the *tepidarium*). It is heated by the overflow from the caldarium. As his body gradually cools down, Marcus lingers in the pleasant water and chats with some of his friends.

Finally, Marcus takes an invigorating plunge into a pool of cold water (the *frigidarium*). This dip is not only refreshing but functional: It closes up his skin pores. Stepping out of the pool, Marcus climbs onto a long table to have his body massaged with olive oil and perfume (for this he has paid extra). Afterwards, refreshed and content, he strolls around the gardens and enjoys the warm Italian sunshine. Isn't this a pleasant way to spend an afternoon?

In 33 BC Rome had 170 baths, and by the time of the Empire there were 1,000! The Emperor Caracalla built the largest complex of baths; it covered thirty-two acres and accommodated nearly two thousand people at one time. The wall surrounding the Baths of Caracalla was over a mile long.

The Theater

Like so many other aspects of Roman culture, the theater was based upon the Greek model. The first Roman

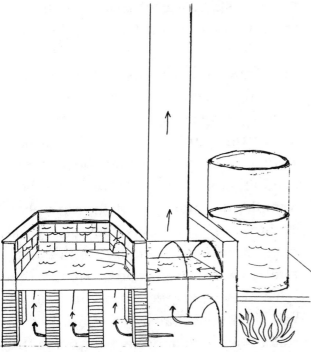

fig. 56 — **The hypocaust system**

dramatist was Livius Andronicus (he was of Greek descent). He lived in the third century BC and wrote Latin versions of Greek plays for presentation at religious festivals. From then on, Roman playwrights continued to copy the characters, plot and story lines of the Greeks.

The Romans preferred comedy to tragedy, and most of their plays had simple themes, such as the kidnapping of a wealthy girl or the clever scheming of a slave. Two comic writers of exceptional talent were Plautus and Terence. Plautus (Titus Macius Plautus, 254-184 BC) wrote a number of amusing comedies that, although they were set in Athens, reflected the intrigues and foibles of contemporary Roman society. Centuries later, Shakespeare would base one of his plays (A Comedy of Errors) on a popular play by Plautus. Terence (Publius Terentius, 195-159 BC) was born in Carthage and brought to Rome as a slave. Fortunately, his master recognized the boy's creative flair and saw to it that he had a good education. Then he freed him. Although Terence also borrowed basic plots from the Greek theater, he developed them into stories that were uniquely his own.

At about this same period Ennius, a Greek poet from Tarentum (239-169 BC) wrote some rather good tragedies (serious plays derived from legends and historical accounts). and once again they were based on Greek works. In the late Republic, playwright Lucius Accius produced Rome's first critical history of drama.

All theatrical roles were played by men (usually Greeks). The actors wore masks made of linen and plaster that were painted to depict such "characters" as a young girl, an old man, or a slave.

In 55 BC Pompey built Rome's first stone theater, a copy of a Greek outdoor amphitheater. The seats were arranged in a semi-circle with the rows sloping down toward a central stage. An awning (the *velarium*) protected the audience from the sun and rain. (Where have you read about a velarium before?) Built into the stage were many ingenious devices, such as trap doors and hoists for lifting actors off stage. The invention of a curtain (it was pulled up from below the stage) made it easy to change scenery between acts.

By this time, special effects had become so important that they superseded all other aspects of the plays. For example, the highlight of the first play produced in Pompey's theater was a procession of six hundred mules that were led across the stage to signify the rich booty acquired after the Trojan War! And high drama was a must. The Greeks had considered it improper to portray an act of violence onstage, and so a death or murder was announced by a messenger in the play (the cries of a victim reverberated from backstage). The Romans, on the other hand, delighted in blood-curdling scenes. Sometimes, for the sake of realism, an actor's place was taken by a condemned man at the last minute, and the poor fellow was actually killed on stage! In lighter scenes, attention was focused more upon the singing and dancing skills of a leading actor than the plot itself, and a comedy often degenerated into slapstick routines and lively acrobatics. Over the years, the Roman theater evolved into a public spectacle of questionable taste; its crude and vulgar portrayals of contemporary life often rivaled the violence and gore of the arena.

Those citizens of the Augustan age who were interested in more refined entertainment could attend the odeons: small (roofed) theaters where poetry was recited. Of course, the wealthy often hired poets and musicians to entertain their guests in the privacy of their own homes.

Latin Literature

We have not yet considered the other literary accomplishments of the Romans. Since most of the great Latin writers lived during the last years of the Republic and the early years of the Empire, now is an appropriate time to briefly examine their major works.

Cicero

The greatest orator of the Republic was Cicero (Marcus Tullius Cicero, 106-43 BC), and he also set the standard for Latin prose. Cicero wrote speeches, essays, and dialogues concerning political matters (he was once a consul and later a supporter of Pompey) as well as religion and ethics. His writing style is characterized by flowing, rhythmical sentences that are enlivened by many descriptive clauses; they contrast markedly with the short precise sentences of his contemporaries. Over eight hundred of Cicero's letters have survived, and they provide a colorful portrait of the social and political happenings of his time. Among his writings are a number of familiar sayings that are reminiscent of Benjamin Franklin's Poor Richard; two examples are "He is his own worst enemy" and "Where there's life there's hope." After all these centuries, human nature has changed very little! Cicero was profoundly influenced by Greek political philosophy, and, in turn, many of his ideas inspired the liberal politicians of the nineteenth century.

The Historians

Among the great Latin writers of the late Republic was Julius Caesar. As we learned, he wrote COMMENTARIES ON THE GALLIC WARS (see page 91) during his military campaign in Gaul. This work is a valuable source of historical material, and it is a fascinating example of early propaganda (Caesar, you will recall, used his writing to win supporters in the political arena). At the same time, it is a fine literary work; Caesar's prose is clear and concise, reflecting the Roman penchant for order.

Livy (Titus Livius, 59 BC - AD 17) was a freed slave who wrote a voluminous history of Rome (in 142 books). This was the first major historical work written in Latin. In many ways, Livy's HISTORY is a companion piece in prose to Virgil's epic about the founding and growth of Rome (THE AENEID), chronicling events up until the reign of Augustus. It was Livy who first wrote down the legend of Romulus and Remus, but he was quick to add that this version of Rome's origin was a fanciful one. His work is extremely patriotic, and although it contains many distortions and inaccuracies, it is filled with descriptive passages that help us to sense what it was like to live in those early times.

Tacitus (Publius Cornelius Tacitus, AD 55-115) is considered by many to be Rome's greatest historian. His major works, HISTORIES and THE ANNALS, cover over seven hundred years of Roman history (through the early Empire) in a straight-forward manner that contrasts with the patriotic and romantic style of Livy. There is, in fact, an undertone of pessimism in his writing and an obvious unease about the decadent lifestyle of the wealthy families of the first century. As we shall soon see, such worries were justified. Tacitus also wrote GERMANIA, a study of the Germanic tribes that were agitating along Rome's northern border.

The letters and essays of Seneca (Lucius Annaeus Seneca, 5 BC - AD 65) provide another glimpse into the everyday lives of the Romans of the early Empire. Although he was a millionaire, Seneca attacked the materialism of the Roman elite, and he complained about the cruelty involved in the public spectacles. Plutarch (AD 46-120) was a Greek living in Rome. His PARALLEL LIVES is a biographical sketch comparing the lifestyles of particular Greek and Roman people. It is an excellent portrait of the times, and it was the source to which Shakespeare turned for historical background when he wrote plays that were set in antiquity.

Juvenal (Decimus Junius Juvenalis, AD 47-128) was a satirist who was offended by the corruption of Roman society. It was Juvenal who coined the term "bread and circuses," and he also wrote the memorable words about the omnipotent Praetorian Guard, "but who will guard the guards?"

Suetonius (AD 70-140) wrote THE TWELVE CAESARS, a rather sensational account of the emperors. Although it is filled with gossip and exaggerations that bring to mind such modern tabloids as THE NATIONAL ENQUIRER, Suetonius' work is still a valuable commentary on the leaders of imperial Rome.

The Poets

Although the Roman culture stressed order, competence and practicality, there were a number of gifted Latins who viewed life in a more ethereal way. They produced a wealth of poetry filled with vivid images that are as evocative today as they were two thousand years ago.

In the first century BC, Lucretius (Titus Lucretius Carus, 99-55 BC) wrote a single major poem entitled ON THE NATURE OF THINGS. Lucretius had earlier been attracted to the Greek philosophy known as Epicureanism. The Epicureans believed that the world was made up of atoms that accidentally came together; thus, human life was purely a natural phenomenon, and a person's soul simply dissipated at the moment of death. This was a far cry from the traditional Roman concept of death! Lucretius wrote his poem to describe this philosophy in poetic terms in the hope of freeing the Roman people from the superstitions and fears traditionally associated with death.

Catullus (Gaius Valerius Catullus, 84-54 BC) was a popular poet living at the time of Caesar and Pompey. He was a keen observer of the human scene, and he wrote many satirical poems that are filled with witty remarks about the general population and the personality quirks of his friends and enemies. He even made fun of Caesar! Catullus also wrote 116 lyrical love poems about his doomed affair with a woman he refers to as Lesbia. (And when Lesbia later turned out to be a scandalously wicked woman, Catullus broke off with her and attacked her venomously in verse!)

Rome's greatest poets were Virgil (Publius Vergilius Maro) and Horace (Quintus Horatius Flaccus). They lived during the reign of Augustus and were greatly influenced by the writers of the Republic. Virgil's early poems about nature and the countryside (THE BUCOLICS and THE GEORGICS) were basically imitations of Greek lyrical works. However, his vast epic poem, THE AENEID, is one of the masterpieces of ancient literature. It was modeled upon the Greek epic poem THE ODYSSEY by Homer. As we learned in Chapter I, THE AENEID describes the adventures of the Trojan prince Aeneas who escapes from the burning city of Troy and eventually founds a new city in Italy. Aeneas, of course, was a Roman superhero: A man of wisdom, courage, integrity, loyalty and devotion to duty. The poem is also a celebration of the struggles and achievements of the Romans. Virgil deftly combined the strands of myth, legend and historical fact to weave a patriotic tapestry of the glory of Rome, ending with the founding of the Empire. (Augustus is presented as a long awaited savior!)

Virgil firmly believed that Rome's destiny was to bring peace, order and harmony to the civilized world. Underlying his praise of everything Roman, however, is a sense of loss of the basic values that prevailed during the early Republic.(Can you list what these were?)

Virgil worked on THE AENEID during the last ten years of his life. He asked his friends to burn the manuscript upon his death, explaining that it was a trivial piece of story-telling. Fortunately, Augustus heard of Virgil's request and, when the poet died, he ordered that the manuscript be preserved and reprinted. (The fact that THE AENEID glorified Augustus and his vast empire must have had a lot to do with this decision!)

Horace (65-8 BC) was Rome's greatest lyric poet. He was the son of a freedman. Horace wrote about such topics as love, beauty, wealth, courage, and death. One of the central themes of his poems is the philosophy expressed in the words *carpe diem* (seize the day)—in other words, take advantage of today because who knows what tomorrow will bring. Over a thousand years later, the English poet Robert Herrick was so moved by Horace's poetry that he wrote his own version of carpe diem, beginning with the famous line, "Gather ye rosebuds while ye may." Horace experimented with Greek cadence and adapted the rhythm of the Latin language to the lyric meters of the Greeks. The ODES, a collection of eighty-eight poems, is considered his greatest work.

Ovid (Publius Ovidius Naso, 43 BC - AD 17) also wrote during the early Empire. His monumental work is METAMORPHOSES; a poetic encyclopedia of Greek and Roman mythology, it is an invaluable guide for scholars of antiquity. Ovid also offered advice for the lovelorn in his two smaller works, THE ART OF LOVE and REMEDIES OF LOVE. These poems reflect many aspects of the social corruption of the upper classes in Rome during the early Empire.

The Volumes

The literary works of the Romans

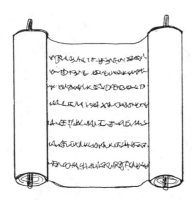

fig. 57 — **A Roman volume**

were written on papyrus, a type of paper made in Egypt from the reeds of plants growing along the banks of the Nile. Pieces of papyrus were glued together and then wound over wooden rollers to form scrolls called *volumenia* (from which our word "volume" derives). If you wanted to read one of these scrolls, you would pull the two rollers apart until the first "page" was visible; to read the succeeding pages, you would simply unroll the papyrus on the right while rolling up the section you've just read on the left. (Think about our modern video tapes—it's the same principle!)

Large numbers of scrolls were copied and sold in Roman bookshops. And, as we have learned, Caesar was so impressed with the library in Alexandria, Egypt, that he ordered one built in Rome. By the fourth century AD there were twenty-eight libraries in Rome alone. As with our modern video cassettes, a person was fined if he did not reroll a scroll before returning it to the library!

Beginning in the second century AD, parchment (dried animal skin) was used in place of papyrus. The parchment was considerably tougher and longer lasting than the fragile papyrus. It was cut in sheets that were bound as a book (called a *codex*). Eventually, most old-fashioned scrolls were replaced by the more practical parchment editions.

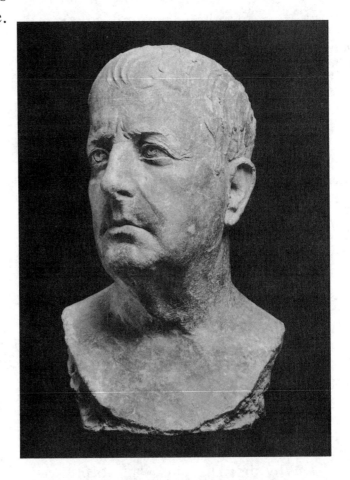

fig. 58 — **Portrait bust of a Roman**
Gift by Contribution — Courtesy, Museum of Fine Arts, Boston

The Fine Arts

Most Roman artists and sculptors were so influenced by the Greeks that their works are usually categorized as "Greco-Roman." (To put it simply, the Roman objects are basically copies of the works of Greek masters.) The major exception to this rule, however, lies with the portrait busts that were made to depict emperors and important statesmen as well as the deceased ancestors in well-to-do families. While the Greek statues usually depicted idealized human bodies, the Roman busts are extremely realistic, showing every wrinkle and line of the subjects they portray. The bas-relief statues (pictures carved in stone) that decorate the arches, columns, tombstones, and temples are also lifelike portraits of the men and women of ancient Rome.

Questions:

1. How did the Colosseum get its name?
2. How did the Romans celebrate the opening of the Colosseum?
3. Describe a race in the Circus Maximus.
4. How did Roman plays differ from Greek ones?
5. Describe the works of Cicero.
6. In what way did the writing of Tacitus differ from that of Livy?
7. Why did Augustus want to preserve THE AENEID?
8. What were volumenia?

Ideas To Think About:

1. Aulus Gellius wrote a story in the first century about a Roman slave named Androcles. According to the tale, Androcles once came upon a lion that was moaning and licking its paw. He examined the paw and removed a thorn. Years later, Androcles was captured and sentenced to die in a public spectacle in the Colosseum. The very lion that he had helped was brought from a cage below and released into the arena. The beast recognized his benefactor and refused to harm him. The Emperor was so moved by what he saw that he ordered Androcles and the lion to be set free. In the years that followed, Androcles traveled from town to town with his lion (on a leash), earning his food and lodging by retelling his unusual story.

2. The Romans discovered their heating system in an interesting way. Sergius Orata was a fish merchant who wanted to raise fish and oysters during the cold of winter. When he elevated his fish tanks on brick posts that arose from fire pits, he was delighted to see that the circulating hot air kept the tanks warm and his creatures healthy! Later, he applied the same principle to human domiciles. He bought up neglected villas and equipped them with heated baths; then he built flues in the walls so that the heat could also circulate

throughout the house. He resold the villas at a considerable profit! Other builders picked up his idea, and before long the Romans were enjoying the pleasures of warm public baths. Homes with "central heating" were extremely expensive, and only the wealthy could afford them.

3. The English word "science" comes from the Latin *scientia*, which means knowledge. For the Romans, science was simply a collection of observations about the natural world. They made no major contributions to man's understanding of the universe; rather, as we have learned, they applied theories developed by other peoples toward practical ends. The Romans did make some contributions to geography, however. Strabo used Caesar's book about the Gallic Wars and other descriptions of Roman territory to write seventeen volumes about the surface of the earth. In 44 BC Marcus Vipsanius Agrippa, a Roman general, was asked by Caesar to survey and map the entire empire. It took thirty years for him to make the map (well into the reign of Augustus) and it was so large that a special building had to be constructed to house it!

In the first century AD Pliny the Elder wrote a huge work on natural history that included a compilation of the Roman knowledge at the time of the fields of geography, zoology, botany, and geology. It is an interesting blend of fact and fiction. In the second century AD Ptolemy (Claudius Ptolemaeus), an astronomer and geographer living in Alexandria, proposed that the sun and the stars circled the earth (this is called the geocentric theory); his mistaken ideas were accepted by most scholars until they were finally disputed by the Renaissance scholar Copernicus.

One Roman who did contribute significantly to science was Galen (Claudius Galenus), the court physician for Marcus Aurelius (see page 127). He wrote a book that described the uses of the parts of the human body and explained the workings of such vital organs as the heart, brain, and kidneys. He also discovered the importance of the spinal cord, noting that paralysis resulted once the cord was cut.

4. The Latin language dates from about seven thousand years ago when the Indo-Europeans moved from the east into central Europe. Over time, local dialects of their language developed among peoples living in different regions. One of these peoples was the Latins (of Latium). Later, as the Roman Empire expanded, the Latin language spread throughout the Mediterranean world. But although Latin was the official language of the Empire, the local tongues did not completely die out. Often the language of a province combined elements of Latin with those of the native tongue.

After the fall of the Empire, the languages spoken in the provinces continued to evolve. In western Europe, this resulted in the creation of the five Romance (from Roman) languages: Italian, French, Spanish, Portuguese and Romanian. The similarities between these languages can be seen in the translations of the English words "good bread": *bonus panis* (Latin), *bon pain* (French), *buon pane* (Italian), *bom pao* (Portuguese), *bun paine* (Romanian), and *buen pan* (Spanish).

When the Normans of France invaded and conquered England in 1066, they brought their Latin-derived language with them. This had a profound effect upon the English language. Today Latin forms the basis of fifty per cent of our vocabulary. Many scientific terms are Latin so that there can be a common terminology for scientists of different cultures. Such everyday words as animal, aquarium, curriculum, exit, formula, index, ultimatum, and vacuum come directly from Latin. And many common abbreviations stand for Latin words: AD (anno domini), AM (ante meridian), c (circa), etc (et cetera), and PM (post meridian).

As we learned earlier, our modern alphabet dates back to the Romans. The Latin alphabet had twenty-three letters; J, U and W were later added. Latin continued to be spoken and written in its pure form in the universities of the Middle Ages, and it remained the official language of the Roman Catholic Church until the 1960's.

Projects:

1. The animal fights in the Colosseum were very bloody, and the creatures involved had little chance for survival. Animal rights activists would be appalled at the carnage. But what about the modern bull fights in Spain? Aren't they just as bad? Write an essay about your feelings about the rights of animals in the modern world. Tie your reasoning in with what you have learned about the animal fights in the Colosseum.

2. Find the poems of Robert Herrick in a book on English poetry. Read the poem that begins "Gather ye rosebuds while ye may." Think about the meaning of the words. Then find a translation of a poem by Horace that treats the same subject. Compare the two works.

3. Given what you've learned about volumenia (and our brief references to Latin words), can you tell the meaning of the name of the popular Swedish-designed family car, the Volvo?

4. Below are some Latin prefixes and roots. Study them, and then make a list of ten words that are derived from Latin. Use each of your words in a sentence.

Examples: prescribe, interfere.

Prefixes:	Roots:
post (after)	clamo (call)
ad (toward)	duco (lead)
cum/con (with)	dico (say)
de (from)	facio (do, make)
e/ex (out of)	fero (bear, carry)
inter (between)	maneo (remain)
intra/intro (within)	mitto (send)
per (through)	porto (carry)
prae/pre (before)	pulso (to hit)
pro (on behalf of)	scribo (write)
re (again)	specto (look at)
sub (under)	surgo (rise up)
trans (across)	voco (call)

5. The Romans admired the Greeks for their achievements in art, philosophy, and literature. Yet, they also harbored a contempt for the Greeks' failings in other aspects of their culture. Find out how the Greek cities were organized before they were conquered by the Romans. Learn about the Greek concept of individual freedom. Then write a short essay explaining what you think might have been the sources of the Roman criticism.

CHAPTER XIII - DAILY LIFE DURING THE PAX ROMANA

The Social Divisions

By the first century AD, Roman society was no longer neatly divided into patricians and plebeians. Marriage between these two groups was common (during the Republic it had been forbidden). Furthermore, plebeians now sat among the patricians as members of the Senate. What mattered most during the early Empire was personal wealth, and a person's family tree no longer determined what he could attain in life. Meanwhile, the gap between the rich elite and the masses of the poor continued to widen.

And then there were the slaves. Every family except the very poor had at least one slave, and the wealthy had dozens. The large estates functioned smoothly because of the labor of hundreds of bonded workers. Slaves could be purchased at public auctions in any city, and there were huge slave markets in Capua and on the Greek island of Delos. Prisoners of war and victims of kidnapping were chained and inspected in these markets as though they were lowly animals. Most slaves performed menial tasks, but the smarter and more capable men became craftsmen, musicians and teachers. A slave was the property of his owner, but, as we have seen, he could win his freedom by good service. The children of freed slaves (called freedmen) became citizens.

Between the two extremes of the rich and poor was a middle class of artisans and merchants, most of whom were freedmen. Although the middle class in Rome was never very large, it had significant numbers in the provinces. It was about this time that the first trade guilds were created. Members of these organizations paid dues, and the money was used for festivals and to cover funeral expenses. Each guild had a patron god or goddess. Of course, the bakers' guild chose Vesta! The Roman tradesmen never considered the possibility of organizing to achieve better working conditions or to raise their wages. That concept was left to later cultures to discover.

The Idle Rich

The upper crust of Roman society—the wealthy landlords—should have been happy. They raked in incredible profits from their vineyards and olive groves and spent them on all kinds of imported luxuries—silk, spices, jewelry, statues, and ostrich feathers, to name just a few. And yet, there was so little for them to do! Since earliest times, the only appropriate work for men of lofty status had been the management of their estates, politics, and the army. But by the first century AD, the large estates were being efficiently managed by specially trained slaves (*procurators*), the once-powerful Senate was only a shadow of its former self, and, since the ardent patriotism of Republican years was long gone, military duty had lost its appeal. So the wealthy became almost as idle as the poor, spending much of their time attending spectacles, lounging around the public baths, and entertaining their friends in a most extravagant manner. Their greatest diversion was plotting against the reigning emperor!

The Cities

The economy of the Roman Empire was based upon agriculture (a staggering ninety percent of the population lived in the country), and the old Republican tradition of the citizen farmer was fondly remembered. Nonetheless, a key feature of Roman civilization was its cities. In fact, the word "civilization" comes from the Latin *civitas* (city) and it means "citified." The cities were the centers of wealth, politics, and entertainment, and city life

is what seems to have mattered most to the writers of the times.

Everyday living conditions did not change radically from the Republic to the Empire, and the cities continued to be noisy, crowded places. The streets of Rome were narrow and winding, because they followed the footpaths of the Latin farmers of centuries past; some had sidewalks and raised stepping stones at the corners so that pedestrians could avoid the mud when crossing from one side to the other. Julius Caesar tried to cut down on city traffic by forbidding carts and wagons on the streets from dawn to dusk. This meant that the merchants had to bring in their produce at night. It must have been difficult to sleep amid the clatter of iron wheels on the cobblestones and the shouting of wagon drivers!

Few Romans could afford private homes, and the majority of the urban population lived in four or five-story tenements arranged in blocks (insulae). The coal-burning braziers used for heating in winter emitted terrible fumes, and the candles and oil lamps that provided the only lighting often overturned and produced fires. The Great Fire of AD 64 swept through the tenements at an unbelievable speed and killed thousands of residents. Although Augustus established Rome's first fire brigade, a relay of men passing leather buckets back and fourth from a water fountain accomplished little when an entire building was in flames. Because of the cramped conditions and the danger of fire, food was often purchased ready-cooked at local bakeries. These were the first fast-food restaurants!

Living in those gloomy, smelly rooms must have been a depressing experience for Rome's lower classes, but at least they were better off than those living in the streets. July first was eviction day. Anyone who had not paid his rent was forced out of his rooms and into the streets on that day.

Contrasting with the squalor of the flimsy tenements were the luxurious city houses of the rich. These were few and far between, averaging one for every twenty-six insulae. They were elegant domiciles, resembling the patrician homes of the Republic but on a grander scale, with high ceilings, wide doors, and stately marble columns. The central atrium was generally two stories tall, and the rooms and gardens often covered an entire block. The outer walls of the houses were constructed of concrete that was faced with brick. The entrance doors had locks and keys to prevent burglary.

Even in these grand residences furniture was sparse, and, as in a Republican domus, the lack of clutter added to the ambience of elegance. The most highly prized household pieces were tables made of rare woods decorated with precious metals and inlaid with ivory or tortoise shell. Some tables had one central leg (these were the most valuable). Beds were simply wooden frames (some were elegantly carved) across which were tacked leather straps. The mattresses were stuffed with straw or wool, and woolen blankets were used on cold nights. The Romans hadn't really thought about sheets. Special couches were used for dining. We'll learn more about them later in this chapter.

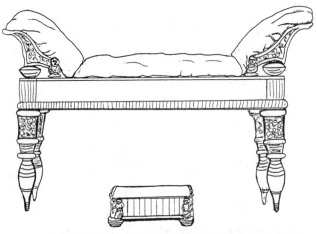

fig. 59 — **Bed and footstool**

The truly distinctive feature of the Roman house of this era was central heating. The same system that heated the public baths was built into the homes of the wealthy. Warm air produced in an underground furnace circulated through ducts in the walls and beneath the floors, making the building quite comfortable in winter. Water entered the house through a lead-lined clay pipe leading from an aqueduct, and a drain carried the waste water off to the local sewer.

When they tired of the noise and pollution of the city, the wealthy Romans retired to their country villas. These lavish homes often contained twenty or thirty rooms. Some very wealthy men maintained several villas (Cicero had owned seventeen!). The Emperor Hadrian, wishing to keep alive his memory of the finest buildings in his empire, had models of them built on his country estate. Throughout his 160 acres there were small versions of Aristotle's Lyceum, Plato's Academy, the Painted Porch of Athens, the temple of Alexander, and numerous Greek theaters and temples as well as Roman baths. There was even an Egyptian canal!

The Role of Women

Roman society was a man's world. We have already learned that the head of the family (the paterfamilias) had great authority. He not only ruled the family, he owned it! He could order the death of a disobedient family member and sell his children into slavery. The Romans loved a figure of power and strength, and the importance of the paterfamilias in their culture helps to

explain why it was easy for the Emperor to exert supreme authority over his subjects.

Although the men made the major decisions, Roman women were free to attend festivals and banquets, and many of them owned property. A few ambitious women went into politics and gave speeches in the Forum, although they could not vote. There were woman lawyers and even lady gladiators!

However, the typical Roman wife spent most of her time at home spinning, cooking and raising the children. Cicero described the ideal woman as "chaste, modest, retiring and faithful." Centuries earlier, one of the Twelve Tables had decreed that "females shall remain in guardianship even when they have come of age," and there was never a time when a woman's life was not controlled by a man: first it was her father, then her husband, and later on (if her husband died) her son or a nephew.

A Roman girl became eligible for marriage at the age of fourteen. Her father selected the man she would marry (love had little to do with it!). Once a wedding contract was drawn up by the two families, gifts were exchanged, and the bride-to-be was given a ring which she wore on the third finger of her left hand. Then the wedding date was chosen. The most popular time to be married was the second half of June (the month named for Juno, patroness of women).

On the day of the wedding, the bride placed her childhood toys by the lararium to symbolize her entry into the adult world. Then she put on her wedding dress: a simple, full-length white tunic, draped with a saffron cloak. Her hair was curled into six ringlets. Attached to her headdress of flowers was a flame-colored veil. The marriage took place in the atrium of her home. After the sacrifice of an animal, the bride and groom signed a marriage contract and joined right hands. A priest then declared them a married couple. (Remember, however, that if the liver of the sacrificed animal was distorted or blemished, the wedding was called off!)

After the wedding feast (including the meat of the sacrificed animal), the groom took his bride to his house. She smeared some animal fat on the doorposts (perhaps a symbol of fertility), and then her new husband carried her over the threshold. (Have you noticed how many of our modern wedding traditions date back to the Romans?) Marriage was not necessarily a permanent institution. By the late Republic, marriage for life had become unfashionable among the upper classes. Julius Caesar had four wives, if you count Cleopatra!

Juno watched over a woman as she gave birth, but it was the father who lifted the baby in his arms and decided whether or not to accept it as his offspring. A frail or sickly baby was often rejected and abandoned on a lonely hillside to die! Sometimes a child was spurned simply because it was a girl. The more fortunate of these abandoned babies were taken home and cared for by other families; usually they became the slaves of their adoptive parents. At the age of nine days, a boy fortunate enough to win his father's acceptance was given his first name, and a bulla (a magic charm) was ceremoniously hung around his neck to protect him against evil spirits. He wore this charm until he was sixteen.

fig. 60 — **Statue of a mother and son**
H. L. Pierce Fund — *Courtesy Museum of Fine Arts, Boston*

Education

The Greeks taught the Romans the importance of education. However, only the boys of privileged classes had formal schooling. (Other children were put to work as soon as they were old enough.) A boy from a wealthy family was entrusted to a well-educated Greek slave (a pedagogue) when he was seven. The pedagogue was responsible for the behavior and appearance of his young charge, and he taught him simple math and grammar.

The next step in the boy's education was to attend an elementary school. This was typically taught by a Greek school-master, usually a freedman who had set up his own school. Any place would do for a school, but it was usually the front room of a house, where the teacher had to compete with the noise and distractions of the city streets. The pedagogues waited in the back of the room.

The students sat upon hard wooden benches and held wax tablets upon their knees. Each boy scratched letters on his tablets with a metal stylus. Afterwards, the wax could be wiped smooth for the next lesson. From dawn to mid-afternoon, with a short break for lunch, the students practiced writing, frequently reciting the names of the letters and chanting the alphabet forward and backwards. When their penmanship was judged acceptable by the schoolmaster, the boys were allowed to practice on papyrus, using a reed pen dipped in a substance made from soot, pitch and octopus ink.

Roman students learned arithmetic by first counting on their fingers and then using a counting frame. The frame consisted of shelves of pebbles arranged in rows which stood for ones, tens, hundreds, and thousands. Our word "calculate" comes from *calculi*, the Latin name for these pebbles. Of course, the boys wrote down the numbers as Roman numerals, and there was no symbol for zero. (See page 161 for a

fig. 61 — **Bust of a young Roman boy**
H. L. Pierce Fund — Courtesy Museum of Fine Arts, Boston

chart of the numerals.) It must have been difficult to add and subtract using such cumbersome symbols. Discipline at the school was harsh, and the rod was frequently used to keep the students on their toes.

At the age of thirteen, a boy graduated from elementary school and entered the grammaticus (secondary school). There he studied the fine points of Latin grammar as well as Greek and read great works of literature. (Every educated Roman citizen was fluent in Greek as well as Latin.) Students often memorized long passages of Virgil and Horace as well as popular proverbs and the original Twelve Tables of Law. They also studied geometry and history.

Although the subject matter was potentially very interesting, the Roman schools were, in fact, rather boring and monotonous. Lessons were taught by rote and drill: Words and numbers were repeated over and over until they were finally committed to memory. The ultimate goal of a Roman education was to become familiar with the inherited wisdom of past generations. Originality and innovation were not encouraged. After all, the Romans excelled at applying established principles, not creating new ones!

Once he completed his work at a grammaticus, a young Roman began a study of rhetoric (the art of public speaking). Since the early Republic, it had been considered essential for a man of noble birth to be a persuasive speaker in the Senate and the law courts.

The final stage of a formal Roman education involved a visit to one of the great centers of learning: A young student might travel to Athens to study philosophy, to Alexandria to study medicine, to Rhodes to further study rhetoric, or to the Athenaeum in Rome to study law, mathematics or engineering. You will recall that Caesar studied rhetoric in Rhodes.

A few wealthy girls were allowed to attend elementary school, but most Roman girls of comfortable means learned everything at home. Some had tutors who taught them about Greek and Roman literature, and nearly all of them learned to dance, play the lyre, and do needlework. The most important part of their education, however, was learning how to direct the household slaves, to supervise the kitchen, and to entertain guests. Girls of lower classes spent their time mastering such practical skills as weaving and cooking.

Roman Dress

The Romans dressed more simply than we do today. The basic men's garment was a cloth (linen) tunic; it was gathered at the waist with a belt so that it fell to the knees (it was considered effeminate to wear it longer). The tunic of a senator had a broad vertical stripe in the center to indicate his rank. In cold weather, a man might wear several tunics at once for warmth; at night, he slept in one of them. Trousers were worn only by soldiers; otherwise, they were the mark of a barbarian!

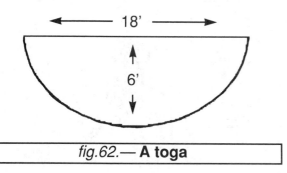

fig.62.— **A toga**

A Roman citizen often wore a woolen toga over his tunic. A toga was simply a length of cloth six yards long and two yards wide; one edge was straight while the other was rounded. As we learned, the toga was a Roman adaptation of the Etruscan robe. Putting on a toga was no easy task. This is how it was done. First, the man threw most of the cloth over his left shoulder; then he pulled it across his back and under his right arm; finally, he threw the end over his left shoulder again. The cloth had to be draped just right. If one end was too short or too long, its wearer became the object of derisive laughter as he walked down the street! Since only a citizen was allowed to wear a toga, it was regarded as a status symbol. If someone was found guilty of a crime in a court of law, he was forbidden to wear his toga. This was considered a terrible punishment!

Beginning in Republican times, a senator, praetor or consul always wore a white toga with a purple hem (a toga *praetexta*) to signify his importance. A censor wore a purple toga (later, only emperors could wear purple togas), and a military hero who had celebrated a triumph wore one that was embroidered with gold. A man running for office wore a toga whitened with chalk. It was called a *toga candida*, from which our word "candidate" is derived. Poor citizens and those in mourning wore dark-colored togas.

The young son of a citizen wore a purple-hemmed toga similar to that of the senior magistrates. At the age of fifteen, he attended a special ceremony in which he exchanged his old toga for a plain one, the toga of manhood (a *toga virilis*). After dedicating the old toga and his bulla (the magic charm he had worn around his neck since infancy) to his household gods, he went to the Forum with his father to officially register as a citizen.

Special tradesmen called fullers cleaned the woolen togas. To do this, they had slaves trample on the garments in tubs containing a mixture of carbonate of soda, potash, and human urine. After this process removed any stains, the togas were rinsed in water and placed out in the hot sun to dry.

The toga was a cumbersome thing. It was not held together with pins, and it was hot and heavy in the summer. Yet, the upper classes tolerated the inconvenience because they thought the garment looked dignified! And, of course, it *was* a status symbol. By the middle years of the Empire, however, togas were worn only for special occasions; the rest of the time, Roman citizens just wore tunics and cloaks. Many a Roman of this period wore his toga only once: when he was laid out for his funeral!

fig. 63 — **Roman dressed in a toga**

A Roman woman wore a *stola*, a loose gown that was pinned with a brooch at her shoulder and fell to her ankles. (She wore a short tunic beneath it.) The stola was brightly colored with vegetable dyes. It was usually woolen or linen, but during the Empire very wealthy women wore garments made from imported fabrics such as silk from China and cotton from India. A cloak called a *palla* was worn over a stola.

fig. 64 —- **A Roman woman**

The Romans loved jewelry, and well-to-do women wore gold and silver earrings, bracelets, necklaces, and rings. Particularly popular during the Empire were cameos: small stones carved with portraits or scenes of everyday life that were worn as brooches or pendants. Roman men who could afford it wore gold rings, many of which were decorated with colorful carved stones.

Standard footwear in Rome was

leather sandals. The senators always wore red ones, and former praetors had crescent-shaped buckles to indicate their status. Children often went barefoot.

Cosmetics and Coiffure

Until fairly recent times, a tanned skin has been the sign of someone who labors outdoors. For this reason, a Roman woman of the privileged class made herself appear pale (and thus aristocratic) by whitening her face and arms with chalk. She highlighted this ghostly make-up by rouging her cheeks and lips with ochre and wine dregs. To condition her skin, she applied a mixture of barley meal and wheat flour, ground antlers, beaten eggs, narcissus, bulbs, gum and honey! She kept her array of toiletries in beautifully carved boxes and glass phials on her dressing table. To protect her delicate skin from the hot Italian sun, she carried a parasol whenever she went outside in the daytime.

Roman men (including the slaves) went each day to a barber to be shaved and, when necessary, to have their hair cut with iron scissors. The shaving must have been painful, since the Romans had no soap. Like today, the barber shop was a busy place and the source of much local gossip. Sometimes a barber put oil and grease on a client's head, hoping to make his hair grow! When the

Emperor Hadrian, perhaps wishing to hide a scar, grew a beard, the look of a clean shaven face went out of style. The men of that time must have been glad to escape the iron blades of the barber each morning.

Fashionable women used curling tongs and ivory combs to prepare the hair styles that became increasingly elaborate during the later years of the Empire. They often wore wigs. When blond-haired Germans were brought to Italy as slaves, the dark-complexioned Romans were so intrigued by "the new look" that light-colored wigs became a big fad.

The lower classes used combs made of wood or bone. These instruments also served a second important function: Lice were prevalent in those days, and the teeth of a comb were ideal for picking the nasty creatures out!

Dining In Rome

Because of the temperate Mediterranean climate, most Romans ate very lightly during the heat of the day. Breakfast was often just a piece of bread dipped in wine and perhaps some fruit or cheese. Lunch (the *prandium*) usually consisted of cold leftovers from the night before, plus a piece of bread and perhaps some olives in a garlic sauce. The *cena* was the main meal of the day. It began around 4 P.M., after everyone had returned from the public baths.

The Romans adopted the Greek manner of eating while reclining on a couch. The dining room was called the *triclinium*, a word meaning "three couches." Each couch had cushions to lean on and accommodated three people. The three couches faced each other in a semi-circle around a low table. Every diner had a particular place to recline which was determined by how important he was (if he was a guest) or by his status in the family. The host or paterfamilias always dined on the left section of one couch (imus) and faced his most important guest who reclined to his immediate left on the adjoining couch. The least important people took their places on the couch furthest from the host. The children sat on stools.

The Romans ate with spoons and their fingers (forks were not invented until the Middle Ages). Toothpicks were placed on the table and freely used. Because so much of the meal was finger food, slaves poured perfumed water over the diners' sticky hands between courses and then handed out linen towels. Guests often brought their own napkins.

The typical family cena lasted several hours. It was a time to share local news and gossip, and everyone lingered until it was time for bed. There was not much else to do in those days after the sun went down! The food was served in three courses and included bread, cheese (made from goat's milk), fruit, vegetables and fish. After one course was completed, the slaves simply removed the central table and replaced it with another one with fresh dishes on it. The Romans also loved eggs, and they probably invented the omelette. The dinner beverage was wine; it was diluted with three parts of water, and even the children drank some. On hot summer evenings, slaves stood behind the couches and fanned the diners with ostrich plumes.

The Roman Banquet

A major form of social entertainment among the wealthy was the seven-course banquet. This was a lavish affair that could last for twelve hours.

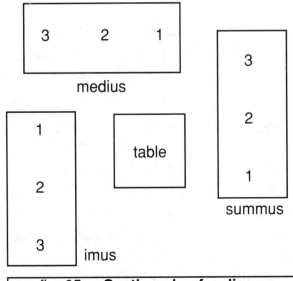

fig. 65 — **Seating plan for dinner**

fig. 66 — **Roman diners**

Families tried to outdo each other by offering the most highly imaginative, mouth-watering dishes to their guests. Of course, the preparation and serving of the food was left to the household slaves.

A banquet always began with a dish of eggs and honey mixed with wine. This was followed by boiled fish, oysters, or snails (that had been fattened on milk). A special delicacy was stuffed dormice baked in honey with poppy-seeds. These tiny rodents were force-fed pine nuts to make them plump and succulent! Rich patés were made from the livers of geese that had been fattened with figs.

The main course consisted of a large number of dishes, the more exotic the better! Here are a few of them: roast boar with spicy radishes, lamprey eel with prawns cooked in olive oil, boiled lobster with asparagus, roasted capon with mushrooms, caviar with sea urchins, sow's udders stuffed with pine nuts and truffles, sauteed nightingale's tongues, and roast fowl—flamingo, stork, ostrich, thrush or peacock. Accompanying the meat dishes were cooked vegetables such as onions, beans, chickpeas, and cabbage.

The Roman cooks created a variety of sauces and seasonings, using such herbs as coriander, oregano, mint, thyme, fennel and sage. Imported spices like pepper, nutmeg, cloves, cardamon and ginger added extra flavor and helped to cover the smell of meat that had been sitting around for hours or days as well as the metallic taste of the lead-lined pots. The only refrigeration in those days was the snow and ice that were imported from the Alps. As you can imagine, it was incredibly expensive.

One sauce could actually be purchased at the market. This was *liquamen*, a kind of fish sauce that was mass-produced and sold in jars just as ketchup and salad dressing are today. Liquamen was made by putting fish gills, blood, and intestines in a large clay pot and then adding salt, wine, herbs and vinegar. This mixture was left in the sun until it turned into an extremely pungent liquid (about two or three months). The result was a strongly flavored fish sauce that was very much in demand by Roman cooks. Can you see why the cooks preferred to buy the liquamen from others and not make it themselves?

The last course of a banquet consisted of fruit (pears, cherries, apples, figs, plums and grapes), nuts, and small cakes saturated with honey. A favorite dish was stuffed dates.

A Roman host could select the wines for his guests from a list of over two hundred varieties. They were classified as black, red, yellow, or white. The best wine came from Campania. Sometimes honey was mixed with white wine to make a sweet beverage called *mulsum*.

We know a lot about the meals of the Romans because of a collection of recipes that have survived from those early times. The recipes are attributed to a man called Apicius Caelius who lived in the fourth or fifth century AD. They have been translated into many modern languages, and many of them are used by modern chefs (with the notable exception of stuffed dormice!).

Roman table manners were rather shocking by modern standards. It was considered polite to belch loudly (thus indicating one's enjoyment of a meal), and it was acceptable to spit on the floor! When a guest had eaten so much that he felt he would burst, he simply excused himself and visited the *vomitorium*. Once relieved of his discomfort, he would return to the table and eat some more!

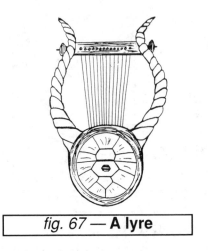

fig. 67 — **A lyre**

The banqueters were always entertained, perhaps by a slave reading poetry or playing a musical instrument. An intellectual host might conduct a literary, philosophical or political discussion with his friends. Less refined banquets often featured dancing girls or even gladiators.

Meals of the Ordinary People

Of course, the poor people of Rome never tasted flamingo or sea urchins. The staple of their diet was wheat from which they prepared bread and porridge. They added herbs, olives, vegetables, or honey for a more interesting taste. There was no butter, but olive oil was often spread on bread. Soldiers in Caesar's army ate porridge nearly every meal, and they complained bitterly when they were ordered to eat freshly killed meat!

Pompeii and Herculaneum

Apart from the writings left to us by

the Romans and the artifacts that have been discovered, much of our knowledge about daily life in those early times is derived from the well-preserved remains of two Italian cities of the imperial period: Pompeii and Herculaneum. They were buried in lava and mud when Mt. Vesuvius erupted in AD 79 (during the reign of Titus).

Pompeii had been a prosperous commercial center and seaport of about twenty thousand people. On the outskirts of the city were many villas, including one that had belonged to Cicero. When the volcano erupted, many people fled for their lives, but others waited, hoping the danger would pass. Slowly and ominously, a thick blanket of white volcanic ash settled upon the city, and the people who remained were overcome by toxic fumes. In the end, nearly two thousand people perished; they were covered by a layer of tiny pumice stones that was ten feet thick. This, in turn, was blanketed with nearly ten feet of ashes.

Some of the survivors returned and tried to dig out their possessions, but eventually the city was forgotten. It lay under its thick blanket for many hundreds of years until it was rediscovered in the sixteenth century. When systematic excavations of Pompeii began in 1748, the archaeologists were amazed to discover that nearly every aspect of the city was perfectly preserved: buildings, pottery, tools, mosaics, frescoes, and pieces of jewelry. There were even petrified loaves of freshly baked bread! Of particular interest were the mounds of volcanic materials that had hardened over the bodies of the victims of the volcano. As a body decomposed, a hollow space was left in its place. Guiseppe Fiorelli, an archaeologist of the nineteenth century, filled in some of these natural molds with plaster. When the plaster hardened, he cut away the pumice surrounding it. He now had an exact model of the body that had once filled the space. How exciting it must have been for him to look upon the figures of men, women, and children who had died in Pompeii nearly two thousand years ago! Since then, plaster casts have been made from the impressions left by most of the human bodies as well as those left by animals, food and even window shutters.

fig. 68 — **Plaster models of a man and a dog**

The city of Herculaneum was a fashionable resort near Mt. Vesuvius. Unlike Pompeii, it was covered with hot mud that hardened. This material was more difficult to cut through than the pumice and solidified ash in Pompeii. Nonetheless, archaeologists have slowly restored many of the remains of the city. So far, each of the two cities has been only partly excavated, so we can look forward to exciting new discoveries being made there in the future.

Questions:

1. Who made up the "middle class" in imperial Rome?
2. How did the rich people spend their time?
3. Describe the city house of a wealthy citizen.
4. Name three wedding traditions that date back to the Romans.
5. What was a pedagogue?
6. What did the boys learn at the grammaticus?
7. What was the correct way to put on a toga?
8. What was the triclinium?
9. What happened to the city of Pompeii?

Ideas to Think About:

1. The Romans associated the color purple with wealth, because the purple dye could only be obtained from the bladder of shell snails that lived off the coast of the Phoenician city of Tyre. One pound of purple wool cost more than the equivalent of $1,000! In the second century AD, the emperor wore a purple cloak to display his lofty position, and it was considered treason for anyone but an emperor to dress completely in purple. Ever since those times, purple has been considered the color of royalty.

2. Gaius Plinius (Pliny the Younger) was a Roman consul. He was seventeen at the time of the eruption of Vesuvius and he was visiting his uncle (Pliny the Elder) near Pompeii. He described the large cloud that rose above the volcano as a huge pine tree that rose from a huge trunk and split into branches. Pliny the Elder was an Admiral of the Roman fleet, and after the initial explosion he ordered his ships across the bay to rescue the victims who were trying to escape the ashes. The falling debris made it difficult to land, and once the Admiral was ashore he determined the seas were too rough to recross the bay. He decided to spend the night on shore at the home of a friend. By the next morning, the ashes and pumice that fell like snowflakes had piled up around the dwellings. Pliny led a group down to the sea, but the waters were still very rough. As he stood wondering what to do next, the Admiral fell to his knees and died, overcome by the poisonous fumes of the ashes. Pliny the Younger wrote a detailed eye-witness account of the

eruption of Vesuvius and his uncle's thwarted rescue attempt.

3. A landmark in the evolution of Roman law, the *Edictum Perpetuum*, was enacted in AD 130. This "perpetual edict" was a codification of most of the edicts that had been made by praetors over the last several hundred years and served as a basis for court decisions. By this time, most inequities and prejudices had been removed, and laws were based upon reason and logic.

Projects:

1. To learn more about the everyday life of a boy in imperial Rome, read DETECTIVES IN TOGAS by Henry Winterfeld (see Readings at the end of this book).

2. THE SECRETS OF VESUVIUS (see Readings) offers an excellent description of what happened in Pompeii in the first century AD. Read the book and make a short report.

3. Roman women, even wealthy ones, led rather restricted lives compared to their modern descendants. Find out more about the daily lives of women of all classes in ancient Rome and write a report. Include examples of women who "went against the tide" and accom-

plished good things in spite of their inferior status.

4. Here is a list of some Roman numerals and their equivalents.

I	one	XXI	twenty-one
II	two	XXX	thirty
III	three	XL	forty
IV	four	L	fifty
V	five	LX	sixty
VI	six	XC	ninety
VII	seven	C	one hundred
VIII	eight	D	five hundred
IX	nine	M	one thousand
X	ten		
XI	eleven		
XIX	nineteen		
XX	twenty		

Study the list. Do you see the logic of this system? Hint: 158: CLVIII; 74: LXXIV; 392: CCCXCII. Now write the following numbers in Roman numerals: 3, 12, 25, 39, 52, 105, 89, 215, 1,783, and 9,812.

5. During the Empire, a vast majority of the Romans were poor; the middle class of artisans, merchants, and (particularly in the provinces) farmers was quite small; and the wealthy elite was an even smaller group. The pyramid in figure 69 roughly illustrates the sizes of the three social groups. Think about the way American society is divided today. Then draw a pyramid that represents the approximate sizes of the lower, middle, and upper classes. Write a paragraph or two explaining why the percentages of people in the different social classes differ from those of ancient Rome.

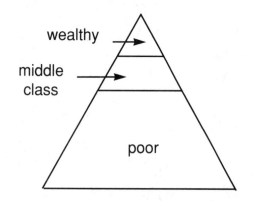

fig. 69 — **The breakdown of Roman society into classes**

6. Here is a good activity for the entire class. Have your own Roman banquet! Fashion clothing out of old sheets and blankets. Arrange pillows to represent dining couches, with trays of food in the center of the triclinium. Reread the section about a banquet, and create a menu of Roman cuisine. Adopt Roman names (Gaius, Lucius, Marcus, Publius, Cornelia, Julia, Calpurnia, etc.) Choose a classmate to entertain the diners with music or witty remarks. Be imaginative, and have fun!

CHAPTER XIV — THE DECLINE AND FALL OF THE ROMAN EMPIRE

The Roman Empire lasted for nearly five hundred years, its extraordinarily efficient systems of law and government determining the lives of millions of people in Europe, Asia and Africa. Yet, every civilization has its flaws, and beginning in the second century AD, a series of political and economic problems began to fester that would eventually undermine the foundations of the Roman state.

Changes Within the Military

Even the invincible Roman army was not immune to internal decay. The make-up of the military had changed greatly over the centuries. As we know, when Marius filled the ranks of the legions with paid fighters, the patriotism shared by the soldiers of the early Republic was replaced by the less lofty view that serving in the army was just a job, like any other. Gone were the days when a farmer picked up his spear and joined his neighbors to drive out an invading enemy. Now a soldier depended upon the Roman state to provide his salary, but his first allegiance was to his commanding officer.

Once the Empire was firmly established, a growing percentage of army recruits came from the provinces, and, as we have seen, even barbarians (primitive tribesmen) were eventually drawn into the ranks. Military positions were often hereditary, a son taking the place of his father on a provincial post. And for the soldiers stationed thousands of miles from the capital city, local politics often took precedence over the decrees of the Emperor.

The Problem of Succession

The stability of the central government during the later years of the Empire was undermined by a lack of formal procedure to select the successor to the throne. In the days of the Pax Romana, either a relative or an adopted heir of the Emperor usually inherited the crown, and so the transfer of power was smoothly accomplished. However, the system malfunctioned when Commodus, the cruel and despotic son of Marcus Aurelius, came to power. After he was strangled by the Praetorian Guard, the title of emperor was passed from one man to another at a very fast pace. On one occasion, the Guard actually sold the throne to the highest bidder! Between AD 235 and 284 there were twenty emperors, and all of them except one suffered a violent death. (In 259 Valerian was taken prisoner by the Persian army—he was the only emperor ever to be captured by an enemy, and he never returned to Rome). One wise emperor allegedly advised his sons, "Stick together, pay the soldiers, and forget everything else."

Fortunately, Augustus had established an efficient bureaucracy of highly trained and well-paid government officials who managed to keep things running for a long time, despite the inadequacies and eccentricities of many emperors.

Financial Woes

The Empire had expanded for the last time during the reign of Trajan, and from then on there were no new sources of plunder to enrich the Roman economy. Furthermore, many of the mines had been worked out, and there was a dearth of raw materials. When the government increased taxes to pay its soldiers, many Roman citizens had difficulty coming up with the money. In 212 the Emperor Caracalla offered citizenship to nearly every male living in the provinces in a gallant effort to increase the number of taxpayers!

The Romans tried to stretch government resources by minting coins that contained increasingly smaller amounts of gold and silver. Eventually, the currency was made up of bronze coins with very thin coatings of the more precious metals. There were still plenty of coins in circulation, but their decreasing value led to terrible inflation. Many people didn't trust the coins at all and resorted to the more primitive system of bartering (exchanging one good for another).

The heavy taxes and growing inflation weakened the once prosperous Roman trade network. Foreign merchants such as the Chinese scorned the Roman coins and demanded gold for their products. Since gold was scarce, they began to take their business elsewhere. To make matters worse, assaults by barbarians living near the Roman borders made merchants increasingly reluctant to travel along the roads in outlying areas. And so, little by little, trade decreased until most people began to rely upon the products of local farmers and artisans.

As economic conditions worsened, thousands of farmers and townspeople living in the provinces abandoned their occupations and joined disgruntled army deserters to form bands of outlaws. They ransacked the countryside, stealing from the unfortunate people who were still trying to make a go of it. Meanwhile, the wealthy landowners looked for loopholes in the system and often paid no taxes at all!

By the late Empire, the number of slaves had dramatically diminished. Since Rome's days of conquest were over, there were no new captives of war, and many former slaves had bought their freedom. This decrease in the slave population meant that there were fewer workers on the large estates. The wealthy landowners remedied this situation by enticing local peasants to become sharecroppers (the peasants farmed the land and had to share part of their produce with the landowners). This system deprived the peasants of most of the rights even the early Latin farmers had taken for granted.

A Decadent Society

Much has been written about the corruption of moral values in imperial Rome. As early as the first century AD, Tacitus complained about the materialism and decadence of the upper classes, and the satires of Juvenal (written a century later) portray Rome as a hotbed of greed and other vices. Even Virgil had lamented how the old values of the Republic had been replaced by complacency and self-gratification.

By the second century AD, there were so few incentives for the wealthy citizens to seek political office that most of them retired to their country estates, leaving the government bureaucracy in the hands of the hard-working equestrians.

Barbarians on the Borders

The population of barbarians living in northern and eastern Europe dramatically increased in the late years of the Empire. As we have learned, Germanic tribes had begun moving from the shores of the Baltic Sea into central Europe as early as 500 BC. Each tribe was made up of many clans who were loyal to a chieftain or king. The men hunted while the women and the slaves (captives of their raids) farmed the land. Since the days of Caesar, the migrations of such nomads had been blocked by legions stationed along the Roman frontier.

Some of these people settled quietly near established farms on the fringes of the provinces and blended in with the local inhabitants. However, when successive waves of barbarians pressed against the northeastern border, the Roman government grew so alarmed that it doubled the size of the army. But this precaution was to no avail; in the middle of the third century an army of Goths burst into Greece and sacked Athens. The Emperor Decius was killed while battling them. Soon afterwards, another flood of warriors, the Franks, invaded Gaul and pillaged everything in sight. Meanwhile, in the east hordes of Arab nomads took over Syria and parts of Asia Minor.

Local trade in these stricken areas of the empire came to a crashing halt as the people living there frantically built protective stone walls around their towns and cities. In 271 the Emperor Aurelian felt compelled to build a huge, protective wall around the city of Rome. It was fifty feet high and eleven miles long; much of it is still standing.

Diocletian

The rapidly disintegrating state of the Empire was temporarily remedied by the Emperor Diocletian (284-305). The son of a freedman, Diocletian restored order by further increasing the size of the army (he hired many German mercenaries) and aggressively fortifying the frontiers. He succeeded in driving back most of the barbarians, which resulted in a welcome but short-lived period of peace. Under his reign, the army took over most branches of the government: Retired soldiers became the governors of the provinces, while other military leaders made key political decisions. The mighty Senate was now little more than a local council for the city of Rome.

To stabilize the economy and prevent further unemployment, Diocletian ordered his subjects to work at their present jobs for life. Sons were compelled to enter the professions of their fathers. He set maximum prices for wages and goods in order to fight inflation. But he also rigorously enforced the collection of taxes, and people of all classes felt the pinch.

The wealthy citizens continued to flock from the cities to their country villas, where they lived in great comfort. Their estates slowly became self-sufficient communities that had little contact with the governing powers of Rome. A landowner could depend upon his peasant sharecroppers to produce an abundant supply of wheat, fruit, and vegetables, while other workers (mostly slaves) tended his herds of cattle, sheep, and goats. The large vineyards and olive groves on his property would keep his family well supplied with wine and oil. And the craftsmen who lived in small villages near the villa could make all the tools and implements he needed. In later centuries, such self-sufficient communities would evolve into the manors of the Middle Ages.

Diocletian realized that the empire had become too large and unwieldy, and so he officially divided it into two halves. As we have seen, there always had been a great difference between the eastern and western provinces; the East was rich, heavily populated, and strongly influenced by the Greek culture and language, while the provinces of the West were relatively primitive. Diocletian further divided the empire into military districts called dioceses to be ruled by vicars. He appointed a co-emperor (a general named Maximian) to rule the western part of the Empire from the city of Milan (what an affront to Rome!), while he personally ruled the East from the city of Nicodemia in Asia Minor. Each emperor bore the title of Augustus. He also appointed an heir for himself and for Maximian, thus providing an easy transition of power in the future. The heirs were given the title of Caesar, and they each governed a sizeable territory. Thus, there were now actually four rulers of the Roman Empire (two emperors and two caesars), although the Emperor of the East was dominant over the other three.

Diocletian then placed the office he held on a higher plane than ever before. Henceforth, emperors were called *domini* (lords), and they claimed direct descent from the gods and heroes of Rome (Diocletian called himself Jovius, the son of Jupiter, while Maximilian was supposedly the protegé of Hercules!). The domini wore golden diadems, purple robes embroidered with gold, and scarlet boots; all magistrates were required to show proper respect by lying prostrate and kissing the hems of the divine purple garments!

Changes in Religion

Many religious changes occurred during the final years of the Empire. Although the traditional sacrifices to Mars and Jupiter were still made for the sake of tradition (and to insure good luck), many of the old Roman gods were nearly forgotten by the second century. There were reasons for this. As we learned earlier, the Roman pantheism (worship of many gods) was basically a system of bargaining with supernatural powers. Priests performed religious rituals whenever it seemed prudent to please the gods (including the spirits of certain dead emperors) while all the worshipers passively looked on. Imagine yourself in such a situation. Would you feel directly involved in a religious experience? Probably not, and neither did most of the Romans. They longed to feel a part of the universal order, and they also yearned to believe in the possibility of their own immortality.

Given the shortcomings of the state religion, many Romans were attracted to the more exotic cults of the eastern provinces. Soldiers stationed in Asia Minor were drawn to the worship of Mithras, the Persian god of light who represented the triumph of good over evil. An initiate into the cult of Mithras was baptized in bull's blood, worshiped in underground temples, and tried to purify himself so that upon his death he would enter a heaven-like realm. Many women turned for comfort to the Egyptian goddess Isis (and her consort Serapis). The cult of Isis was based upon the cycle of life, death and rebirth. These eastern religions appealed to the emotions in a way that the Roman religion did not, and they fostered the hope that, despite the hardships of this life, something better lay ahead.

The Life of Jesus

During the first century AD, a new religion sprang up in the eastern empire that would ultimately have a profound effect upon the entire civilization of Rome. This new religion was Christianity. It began in Judea (modern Israel), a part of Palestine. When Palestine became a Roman province in the first century BC, it continued to be ruled by Jewish kings (who acted with the consent of Rome); eventually, however, the kings were replaced by Roman governors.

Jesus was a Jew born in Judea near Jerusalem during the reign of Augustus. At this time, the local government was completely in the hands of the Romans. As a boy, Jesus carefully studied the sacred writings of the Jewish prophets. He grew up to become a carpenter, but his great interest lay elsewhere. When he was thirty, Jesus began to travel around the countryside preaching to the ordinary people living in small villages. He believed that he was the son of an all-powerful God, and he offered a message of hope and salvation to the crowds who gathered to hear him. Jesus said that God loved all mankind (whom He had created), and He even forgave those who committed sinful acts, as long as they were truly sorry for what they had done. Jesus called upon his listeners to follow His example, to be loving and forgiving of each other; and he promised that a good life would be rewarded with immortality of the spirit.

Jesus' teachings were in keeping with those of the Jewish prophets who had lived in earlier times. He spoke simply in the language of the common people, and he illustrated his message through stories called parables. This made it easy for his listeners to understand his religious ideas, and he attracted many followers, particularly among the uneducated classes.

The Jews living in Palestine resented the occupation of the Romans. They disliked the high taxes they were forced to pay, and they refused to acknowledge the divine status of Roman emperors. Many of them hoped for a "Messiah"—someone who would liberate them from their overlords. When Jesus and twelve of his followers (called the Disciples) arrived in Jerusalem to celebrate Passover (the holiday marking the exodus of the Jews from Egypt), many Jews greeted him as the Messiah they had been waiting for. Others, however, were skeptical of Jesus' claim to be the son of God, and they accused him of blasphemy. Pontius Pilate, the Roman governor of Judea, had been angered by the Jewish resistance to the Roman occupation, and he was looking for ways to end the disturbance. He seized upon the occasion of Jesus' condemnation by a Jewish ecclesiastical court to order his execution. Pilate hoped that by making an example of Jesus, he would force the more recalcitrant Jews to accept Roman authority. Jesus was crucified. This was the common form of execution for non-citizens and slaves: The arms and legs of the victim were bound or nailed to a wooden cross, and then he was left to die slowly (and painfully).

The Disciples claimed that after Jesus was buried, his body disappeared from the tomb, and that he then miraculously appeared to them on numerous occasions. Jesus told them, they reported, that he had given his life in order to obtain God's forgiveness for the sins of all humanity. After forty days, Jesus disappeared and (the Disciples said) ascended to heaven. This convinced them that he was indeed the Son of God.

The Spread of Christianity

After Jesus died, the Disciples tried to spread his teachings throughout Palestine. However, since most Jews there wanted a political Messiah rather than a religious one, they took their message to other lands. Paul of Tarsus (in Asia Minor) was a Disciple who believed that the message of Jesus was intended not only for Jews but for all mankind. He said that Gentiles (non-Jews) could become followers without having to accept the laws and rituals of the Jews. They simply had to believe in Jesus. This attracted many non-Jewish converts who had been unwilling to embrace Judaism. Jesus was given the name Christ (from the Greek word *Christos* meaning Messiah). His followers were therefore called Christians.

Christianity (the religion of the Christians) contrasted dramatically with the materialism of contemporary Roman society; it proposed humility, charity and brotherhood in place of greed and self-interest. Paul and other Disciples took the new religion to Asia Minor and Greece where they founded small Christian communities called "cells." Paul later went to Rome and devoted his time to preaching and organizing a cell there. His letters make up the oldest part of the New Testament of the Christian Bible.

The Roman Resistance to Christianity

By AD 100 there were Christians living in most of the major cities in the Roman Empire, although they constituted a small minority of the total population. At first, many Romans confused Christianity with Judaism, but by the time of Nero they grasped the fundamental difference between the two religions. Their were times, however, when they totally misconstrued the actions of the Christians. For example, they worried that by meeting in private houses (there were no churches at that time), the Christians were plotting against the Emperor. And the Communion Service, in which bread and wine were consumed as symbols of the body and blood of Christ, led a few hysterical and poorly informed Romans to conclude that Christians were cannibals!

For their part, the Christians actively incurred the wrath of the Romans by refusing to serve in the army or to hold public office; furthermore, they criticized their pagan festivals as well as the institution of slavery. They also complained about the cruel sports that took place in the public arenas. Some Romans worried that by offending the gods, the Christians were causing all sorts of disasters. And they could not understand the Christians' refusal to accept the divinity of Roman emperors.

The Persecutions

When Nero blamed the Christians for causing the great fire in Rome in AD 64 (see page 124), he began a period of persecutions that would last for over two hundred years. Nero ordered his Guard to round up all the Christians they could find, and these innocent people were executed in terrible ways. Some were covered with animal skins and sent into the arena of the Colosseum to be torn apart by ravenous dogs. Others were nailed to crosses and then set afire. Among Nero's victims were the Disciples Peter and Paul. For years to come, the Christians provided entertainment for the Romans as they desperately tried to escape the teeth and claws of wild animals in the arenas of most major cities. The Emperor Diocletian made it a criminal offense to be a Christian and stepped up the persecution of the so-called "atheists."

From the beginning, the Christians had been forbidden to use regular burial places, and so they buried their dead in crowded underground tombs outside of Rome called catacombs. With the enforcement of the stricter laws of Diocletian, they began to use the catacombs for services. This, of course, made the Romans even more suspicious!

Yet, in spite of the persecutions and harassment of Christians by the Roman authorities, the new religion continued to appeal to people from all walks of life, the rich as well as the poor. By the dawn of the fourth century, one out of every ten Romans was a Christian.

Constantine

After the death of Diocletian, his government ceased to function efficiently; too many ambitious men became embroiled in the fight for the titles of Augustus and Caesar. This conflict was finally resolved in 312 at the Battle of the Milvian Bridge when Constantine, the son of a former Caesar, triumphed over his competitors. According to legend, on the eve of the battle Constantine thought he saw a cross in the sky with the inscription "with this sign you will conquer." That night he had another vision in which he was told that by painting a cross on the shield of each of his soldiers he would win the battle. When he awoke the following morning, he ordered the shields painted. Guess who won the battle!

Constantine selected strong leaders among his followers to help him govern the sprawling empire, but differences of opinion about state policy led him to appoint himself sole Emperor in 324. He moved the eastern capital to Byzantium, which he rebuilt and renamed Constantinople (after himself). This city, which Constantine referred to as the "new Rome," was strategically perched above the entrance to the strait linking the Black Sea to the Mediterranean.

Constantine continued Diocletian's policy of permanently tying workers to their jobs and requiring that sons take up the trades of their fathers. Many Roman citizens complained that they were little more than prisoners of their government, but there was little they could do about it. Imagine their despair when they realized that as the quality of their lives declined, the court of the Emperor had become more elaborate!

His victory at the Battle of the Milvian Bridge convinced Constantine of the power of the cross. In the Edict of Milan (an official proclamation) of 313, he reversed the state religious policy by declaring that the Roman people could worship any god (or gods) they wanted. He encouraged the growth of Christianity by building churches in Rome and Jerusalem. Although the political status of Rome had dwindled, the city on the Tiber became the spiritual center of the Christian Church. Constantine allotted government money for the support of Christian schools, and he raised new taxes specifically for the Church. Christian leaders who took on government jobs were exempt from taxation. Just before he died in 337, Constantine was baptized as a Christian, thereby uniting the office of the Roman Emperor with the Christian Church.

In 395 the Emperor Theodosius made Christianity the state religion of Rome, and he outlawed all other faiths. It became a crime to offer flowers or incense to the household gods whose statues graced the family lararium. Gladiator fights were abolished in 404 after a Christian monk named Telemachus was stoned to death by angry spectators in the Colosseum when he tried to separate two combatants. In 408 an official decree ordered that all pagan temples must be used for non-religious purposes, and large Christian churches were built in the major cities.

The Organization of the Christian Church

Like the Roman government, the organization of the Church consisted of an intricate network that connected each local unit to a centralized leadership. At the community level, a church under the guidance of a priest was called a parish. A group of parishes made up a diocese (remember the military divisions of Diocletian?). Each diocese was headed by a bishop. Those bishops whose dioceses included major cities were called archbishops. The archbishops who governed Rome, Milan, Constantinople, Antioch and Jerusalem became very powerful. They were called patriarchs (fathers).

In the fifth century the Bishop of Rome would claim authority over the other archbishops (although the eastern patriarchs never recognized his authority). He became known as the Pope. In this way, the ancient Roman concept of the paterfamilias was preserved in the organization of the church. In modern times the Bishop of Rome still heads the hierarchy of the Roman Catholic Church.

The Continuing Threat At the Borders

As the Christian Church grew in power, the empire itself became more and more fragmented. Land along the northern frontier, which had been under constant assault from warrior tribesmen, was finally lost when large numbers of barbarian mercenaries defected from the legions and used their Roman weapons against their former allies. After Theosodius died in 395, the empire broke into two halves again. While the eastern half, ruled from Constantinople, remained stable and strong, the western part grew steadily weaker.

Troubles continued to brew along the borders in eastern Europe. The Huns, ferocious nomadic horsemen from Mongolia, were the most feared of all the barbarians. As they migrated westward from Asia, they conquered the

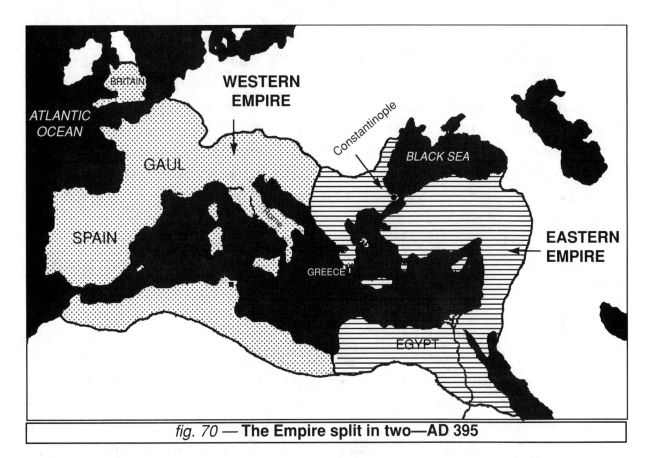

*fig. 70 — ***The Empire split in two—AD 395**

Ostrogoths (Goths of the eastern region) and drove the Visigoths (Goths of the western region) across the Roman frontier at the lower Danube River. While the astonished Romans watched, over two hundred thousand frightened refugees fled across the water. Valens, the Emperor of the East, granted these people official permission to settle there and even promised them protection. But the local farmers were not happy with their new neighbors, and the barbarians themselves were unprepared to pay the taxes demanded of them by the Roman government. Some of them were obliged to sell their own wives and chil-

dren into slavery in order to come up with the money! In 378 the unrest erupted into fighting: The Visigoths attacked the Romans, killing Valens and most of his legion. According to the peace agreement that was negotiated, the Visigoths were allowed to remain in the region, but on their own terms. The Romans made the most of the situation by hiring the tribesmen to protect the border against other barbarians. They even made the Visigoth king a Roman General!

But in spite of such attempts to compromise with the barbarians, there seemed to be no end to the raids along the border. And so, little by little, the western half of the empire crumbled. In 407 the Roman troops were recalled from Britain, leaving that island in the hands of other Germanic tribes—the Saxons, Angles and Jutes. There were fewer problems in the provinces of the East, since they bordered the lands of the Persians and other civilized peoples who did not have the same desire for new territories as the barbarian tribesmen.

The Sack of Rome

In 406 the Rhine River froze, enabling a tribe called the Vandals to cross into Gaul. They ravaged the countryside (the Roman legions could do little to stop them) and then invaded Spain. A few years later (410) the Visigoths, led by a wily chieftain named Alaric, actually arrived in Rome. This was the first time a foreign army had entered the proud city on the Tiber since the invasion by the Gauls in 390 BC. It was a humiliating blow for the Romans. The senators sadly acknowledged that the local population could no longer rely upon them for money or direction. In despair they announced, "You are on your own."

At this time, the most important man in Rome was the Bishop; he met with Alaric and told him to do as he wished with the local treasures but pleaded that he spare the lives of the people. Can you imagine Caesar doing something like that? For two days Alaric's men ransacked the city that had once been the heart of a mighty empire. Then they moved on to Spain, where Alaric drove out the Vandals and established his own territory.

Attila the Hun

In the middle part of the fifth century the leader of the Huns was Attila. He was unquestionably one of the most infamous villains of history. In 434 Attila and his brother (Bleda) had negotiated a treaty with Theodosius II, the Emperor of the East, in which he agreed to keep off Roman lands in return for an annual tribute of seven hundred pounds of gold. This was a huge amount of gold, and the fact that the impoverished Romans were willing to pay it indicates how desperately they wanted to keep the Huns at bay. But after six years of peace, Attila grew restless and crossed the border, destroying several important cities and defeating the imperial troops. Once again, the Romans bought him off by increasing the amount of tribute.

In 445 Attila murdered his brother and launched a new campaign against the Empire. He reportedly announced that he intended to conquer the whole world. He attacked the Roman army and forced the Emperor not only to increase the tribute once again but also to cede to him large areas of territory south of the Danube River. By this time, the pattern must have become agonizingly clear to the Romans!

Luckily for Theodosius, Attila's interest shifted toward the western half of the Empire. In 450 he crossed the Rhine River and marched toward Gaul. Aetius, the Roman general in Gaul, solicited the support of the barbarians already living there. United by a common fear of the blood-thirsty Huns, an unlikely army made up of Romans, Visigoths and other local tribesmen stopped Attila in his tracks near Orleans and drove him back. Aetius' decisive defeat of the Huns at the Battle of the Catalaunian Plains (451) was the last great victory for a Roman general.

Angry yet determined to continue his conquest of Roman lands, Attila led his men south into Italy, where they ravaged the Po valley. His disregard for human life and property in his continuous assaults upon Roman territories earned him the title "the Scourge of God." When he reached the city of Rome, he was apparently bought off by the Bishop (Pope Leo I). Soon afterwards, an epidemic broke out and Attila withdrew to the north. The next year (453) he died. Without his evil leadership, the Huns were no longer a threat to Rome. They eventually settled on the plains of modern Hungary.

More Invasions

Meanwhile a Vandal chieftain, Gaiseric, crossed the strait of Gilbraltar and invaded the Roman territory in North Africa. He gradually gained control of the western Mediterranean, and in 455 he, too, sacked the city of Rome. The Vandals were extremely warlike and destructive, and their vicious assault upon Rome resulted in the coining of a Latin term from which the English word "vandal" is derived. (A vandal is someone who causes senseless damage and destruction.) For two weeks, they ransacked and plundered the buildings of Rome, loading tons of valuable objects on their ships in the port of Ostia. Once again, Pope Leo tried to negotiate with the invaders, but this time he could only obtain the guarantee that citizens would not be killed unless they resisted.

Meanwhile, the Franks had gained control of most of central and northern Gaul. Ever since, Gaul has been known as the land of the Franks (France).

The End of the Western Empire

By the second half of the fifth century, the western emperors, who until then had continued to wield some power and authority from their new capital of Ravenna, were little more than puppets controlled by the barbarian leaders. The end came in 476. In that year, a barbarian chieftain named Odoacer deposed Romulus Augustulus, the last Roman emperor of the West. The mighty Roman Empire that had dominated the Mediterranean world for hundreds of years was no more. One of the ironies of history is that the name of the last Emperor combines those of Rome's first king (Romulus) and first Emperor (Augustus).

Odoacer ruled the territory surrounding Rome for fifteen years. After his death, a group of Ostrogoths led by Theodoric invaded and conquered Italy.

Afterwards

By 500 all the former western provinces had become independent kingdoms ruled by the barbarians: the Ostrogoths in Italy, the Franks in Gaul, the Visigoths in Spain, the Vandals in Africa, and the Saxons, Angles, and Jutes in Britain. With no central bureaucracy to oversee their upkeep the roads, buildings and aqueducts fell into disrepair. There was no standard currency, and so everyone resorted to bartering for goods. Throughout western Europe, the surviving Roman landowners who had retired to their country villas became the feudal lords of small independent city-states, while the majority of the people toiled as peasants.

The period following the fall of the western empire is called the Dark Ages, because most people living in Europe then were illiterate; many of the Roman innovations in government, law, and technology were nearly forgotten. But it is important to remember that the Germanic invasions did not destroy the Roman Empire—they simply speeded up a process that had begun much earlier with the gradual deterioration of the framework of Roman society.

Fortunately, amid the darkness there was a flicker of light. The Christian Church not only survived in the west, it became the center of order and stability. The system of laws practiced within the Church, called the Canon Law, was founded upon Roman legal procedures. Latin was maintained as the official language of the Church and used in all services until the twentieth century. And the libraries of the monasteries preserved the ideas of the greatest minds of Rome.

Writings of the Early Church

Jesus left no writings, but his Disciples wrote much about his life and teachings. At the end of the fourth century, the accounts of four Disciples (Matthew, Mark, Luke and John) were accepted as part of the official teachings

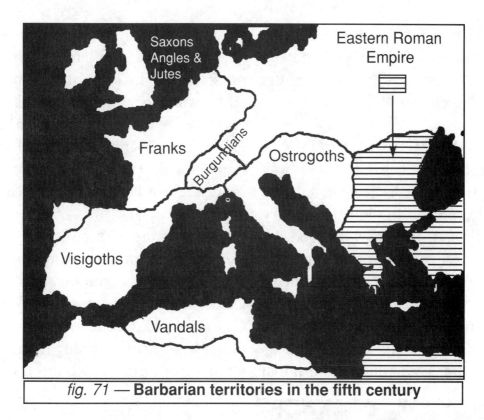

fig. 71 — **Barbarian territories in the fifth century**

of the Christian Church. Together with letters written by Paul and other Christian writers, they made up the New Testament of the Bible. They were written in Greek.

Between 100 and 500 AD scholars of the Church (known as the Church Fathers) added to the ever-growing Christian literature. In the fifth century, one of the Fathers, a man named Jerome, translated the Old and New Testaments from Greek into Latin; this work (called the Vulgate) became the official Bible of the Roman Catholic Church.

A contemporary of Jerome was Augustine, an influential philosopher-theologian who wrote a Christian interpretation of history entitled THE CITY OF GOD. In his work, Augustine defended Christianity against a common charge of his day, namely that the Christians had caused the decline of Rome by turning the citizens away from the traditional gods. Augustine proposed that Rome's fall was a punishment for the selfishness and materialism of its society as well as the persecution of the Christians. He concluded that Rome would have fallen eventually, whether there were Christians or not, and that the only eternal city was the City of God, which lies in the realm of faith. Augustine also wrote an autobiography,

THE CONFESSIONS, which describe his quest for meaning in life and his discovery that the answers reside in the Christian Church.

The Byzantine Empire

We must remember that it was only the western half of the Roman Empire that came to an end in the fifth century AD. The Eastern Empire withstood the onslaught of the barbarians, and the Greco-Roman culture continued to thrive there for another thousand years. Historians refer to the civilization of the Eastern Empire during this period as Byzantine, after Byzantium, the original Greek name of the city of Constantinople.

Emerging as the largest, richest, and most beautiful city in Europe, Constantinople became the center of the civilized world. It preserved Greek learning and Roman political innovations. Greek-speaking Christians living in the eastern Empire acknowledged the supremacy of the Archbishop of Constantinople (the counterpart of the Pope). For centuries, the Byzantine Empire fostered the development of Christianity in the Eastern Orthodox Church, preserved the writings of church scholars in the libraries in Constantinople, and encouraged the

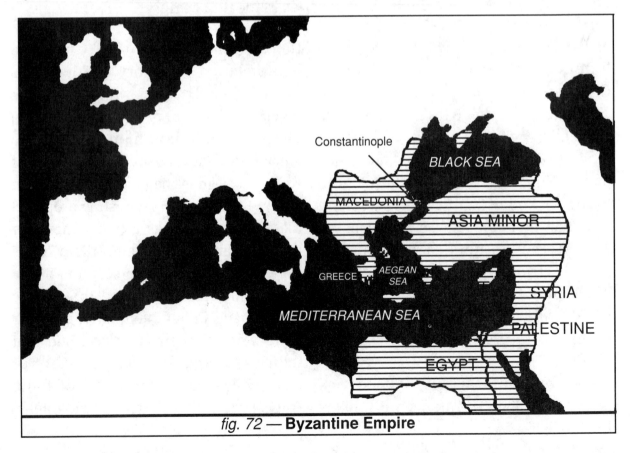

*fig. 72 — **Byzantine Empire***

growth of trade as well as the evolution of a new and unique style of art. The Byzantine Empire came to an end in 1453 when the Turks sacked its capital city.

Questions:

1. How did some of the emperors try to deal with inflation?
2. Why did the number of slaves decrease?
3. Who were the Goths?
4. What are three ways that Diocletian tried to restore order to the empire?
5. What was the central message of Jesus' teachings?
6. Why were so many Romans attracted to Christianity?
7. Why did Constantine convert to Christianity?
8. List five adjectives that describe Attila the Hun.
9. Compare and contrast the western and eastern halves of the empire after Theodosius.

Ideas To Think About:

1. Justinian ruled the Byzantine Empire from 527 to 565. He tried to regain parts of the former western empire, and he succeeded in winning back North Africa from the Vandals, Italy from the Ostrogoths, and southeastern Spain from the Visigoths. Unfortunately, all the land he had acquired was lost again by his successors.

More significantly, from a modern point of view, Justinian appointed a committee to revise the Roman laws. Material had been accumulating for a thousand years, and the legal system had become not only unwieldy but self-contradictory. The committee clarified and codified the laws. The result was the Justinian Code, and it became the basis for the modern legal systems of many parts of modern Europe, Japan, and the United States.

2. According to tradition, the Christian Church in Rome was founded by a man named Peter, one of Jesus' original Disciples. He was later crucified upside down in the Vatican Circus (hippodrome) during persecutions ordered by Nero. The place where he died became the site of the Cathedral of St. Peter (in the center of what is now the smallest country in the world, Vatican City). The line of the Bishops of Rome in the Catholic Church (the Popes) extends back to Peter.

3. Many causes have been proposed for the fall of the Roman Empire. A declining birth rate, increased cases of malaria (it was impossible to fully drain the swamps), and the lead lining the pipes of the aqueducts all contributed to a dramatic decrease in the population at a time when more men were needed to defend the borders. The historian

Gibbon asserted in his famous work THE DECLINE AND FALL OF THE ROMAN EMPIRE that Christianity was the major cause of the fall of Rome (Augustine notwithstanding!).

4. Although Rome became the spiritual center of the empire and later the center of the Catholic Church, many of the vestiges of its former political grandeur were ignored. In fact, the ancient monuments that once reflected the power of the Romans were treated as quarries, and the stones were used for new buildings. And just imagine: The Forum became a cow pasture! The port city of Ostia was abandoned in the fourth century AD because of an epidemic of malaria as well as the silting up of its harbor.

Projects:

1. Do you think the fall of the Roman Empire was a good thing? After all, it wiped out political despotism and ended the union of church and state. Think about how the fall of Rome affected Europe. What were conditions probably like there during the Dark Ages? Write a short report explaining why you think the fall of Rome benefitted mankind (or why it didn't!).

2. Some causes for Rome's downfall have been proposed that seem relevant to other, more modern cultures. For example, it has been suggested that the Romans' acquired taste for beef during the years of the Empire brought about the collapse of the economy; this is because each animal ate a tremendous amount of grain, and this drove up the price of wheat to an extremely high level. Other scholars have proposed that the barbarians who invaded the frontiers brought with them new diseases to which the Roman people had little immunity. Think about these possible causes of Rome's downfall. Then, select one of them and write several paragraphs explaining how the same problem affected another, later culture. (For example, what was the effect of the arrival of European settlers upon the health of the Native Americans?)

3. The Turks sacked Constantinople two years after the birth of Christopher Columbus. What is the historical significance of each of these two events? What is interesting about the fact that they occurred at nearly the same time? Write a short report.

CHAPTER XV — THE LEGACY OF ROME

Julius Caesar once said that the Romans eagerly copied any good idea, whether it was from a friend or an enemy. As we conclude our study of their ancient civilization, we can certainly appreciate the truth of Caesar's remark!

From earliest times, when Rome was little more than a few clusters of huts on the hills overlooking the Tiber, the industrious Latins made the most of their environment and adapted any techniques or concepts that improved the quality of their lives. Roman culture was immeasurably enriched by the engineering skills of the Etruscans, the religious beliefs of the Greeks, the ship design of the Carthaginians, the guerrilla war tactics of Hannibal, the steel making process of the Spanish, and the recipe for cement devised by the Egyptians. And this was only the beginning!

The Romans were master politicians. We have seen how they ingeniously made loyal citizens of their former enemies. A willingness to compromise reinforced by a fervent determination to make things work enabled the Romans to devise the framework of the Republic and then to transform it into the vast bureaucracy that efficiently ruled the world's largest empire for centuries.

A detailed record of cases formed the basis of Roman law, and, from the start, the emphasis was upon the rights of the individual. Nor was a person condemned to punishment unless he was first proven guilty. This continues to be a hallmark of most systems of justice throughout the modern world.

Respect for tradition and authority were central to the Roman way of life. The concept of the paterfamilias gradually evolved from the the days of tribal chieftains of Latium, and it helps to explain why the Romans accepted the autocratic rule of the later emperors. It also played a key role in the highly disciplined and nearly invincible Roman army.

Our own culture owes much to the systems of government and law created by the Romans two thousand years ago. But there are so many other aspects of our lives that are also linked to those early times. Some we've learned about are the Roman numerals on a clock face or in a book's table of contents, the letters of the alphabet, and the names of the months of the year. Half of the words in the English language come from Latin. Think about Nero when you next eat a dish of ice cream (he invented it!) or the Roman cavalry when you pick up a lucky horse shoe (their gallant steeds wore removable "hipposandals"). Remember Sergius Orata, the inventor of the hypocaust system of heating, whenever you sit in a hot tub or sauna. And think of Jupiter the next time your grandfather remarks, "By Jove!" (Jove was Jupiter's nickname!)

Roman architects would be pleased to see their basic designs reflected in today's world: the dome of the capital building in Washington, D.C., Dodger Stadium in Los Angeles, the Astrodome in Houston, St. Patrick's Cathedral in New York, and the subways in our major cities are but a few examples of the modern use of Roman engineering techniques. The towns that sprang up at important junctions of Roman roads or that grew around army barracks are today bustling cities; among them are Marseilles, London and Naples. And you can still walk along the Appian Way.

Perhaps the most important legacy of ancient Rome can be found in the words of the historians of those early times. It has been said that those who don't learn from the mistakes of the past are condemned to repeat them. By studying the detailed descriptions of the political, social, and economic developments of the Roman Republic and Empire, we can better understand what went wrong and hopefully avoid similar pitfalls in our own society.

Ideas To Think About:

1. Unlike Roman citizens, Americans are represented in their central government by legislators they have elected. Perhaps had the Romans considered the possibility of creating a multi-national assembly made up of delegates from all the provinces to formulate national policies, they might have strengthened the foundations of their society and staved off the decline and fall of the Empire.

2. We have learned that the Romans were conservative people. They revered their past and looked backwards rather than forwards. Scholars living during the fourteenth and fifteenth centuries would rediscover the ancients and take the ideas of such great thinkers as Cicero and even Augustine further than the Romans ever could. They could do this because they were not hampered by a blind devotion to longheld traditions as the early Romans had been.

Projects:

1. "Conquered Greece held her proud conqueror captive." These are the words of Horace. Write a short report explaining what they mean.

2. Make a collage of pictures of buildings and other structures that reflect Greco-Roman culture. Look in magazines for arches, colonnades, amphitheaters, and so forth. Travel brochures are an excellent source of photos.

3. What do *you* think was Rome's greatest contribution to western culture? What was its greatest weakness? Write a short report discussing your answers to these questions.

SUGGESTED READINGS

Amery, Heather and Patricia Vanags, TIME TRAVELLER BOOK OF ROME AND ROMANS, London: Usborne Publishing Ltd, 1976.

Ballard, Robert, THE LOST WRECK OF THE ISIS, Toronto, Canada: Madison Press, 1990.

Bisel, THE SECRETS OF VESUVIUS, Toronto, Canada: Madison Press Books, 1990.

Burrell, Roy, THE ROMANS, Oxford, England: Oxford University Press, 1991.

Cairns, Trevor, THE ROMANS AND THEIR EMPIRE, Cambridge, England: Cambridge University Press, 1987.

Connolly, Peter, THE ROMAN ARMY, Englewood Cliffs, NJ: Silver Burdett, 1985.

Connolly, Peter, THE LEGIONARY, London: Oxford University Press, 1988.

Connolly, Peter, HANNIBAL AND THE ENEMIES OF ROME, Englewood Cliffs, NJ: Silver Burdett, 1985.

Corbishley, Mike, THE ROMAN WORLD, New York: Warwick Press, 1986.

Forman, Joan, THE ROMANS, Englewood Cliffs, NJ: Silver Burdett, 1985.

James, Simon, ANCIENT ROME, New York: Alfred Knopf, 1990.

James, Simon, ANCIENT ROME, New York: Viking, 1992.

MacCaulay, David, CITY, Boston: Houghton Mifflin, 1974.

Miquel, Pierre, LIFE IN ANCIENT ROME, Englewood Cliffs, NJ: Silver Burdett, 1985.

Ochoa, George, THE ASSASSINATION OF JULIUS CAESAR, Englewood Cliffs, NJ: Silver Burdett, 1991.

Odijk, Pamela, THE ANCIENT WORLD; THE ROMANS, Englewood Cliffs, NJ: Silver Burdett, 1989.

Place, Robin, THE ROMANS; FACT AND FICTION, Cambridge, England, Cambridge University Press, 1988.

Rutlins, Jonathan, SEE INSIDE A ROMAN TOWN, London: Kingfisher Books, Ltd., 1986.

Usher, Kerry, HEROES, GODS AND EMPERORS FROM ROMAN MYTHOLOGY, New York: Schocken Books, 1984.

Wilkes, John, THE ROMAN ARMY, Cambridge, England: Cambridge University Press, 1989.

Winterfeld, Henry, DETECTIVES IN TOGAS, San Diego: Harcourt Brace Javonovitch, 1990.

Videos:

BEN HUR
CLEOPATRA
I, CLAUDIUS
JULIUS CAESAR
SPARTACUS

INDEX